CONCILIUM

concilium 1999/3

THE NON-ORDINATION OF WOMEN AND THE POLITICS OF POWER

Edited by

Elisabeth Schüssler Fiorenza
and Hermann Häring

SCM Press · London
Orbis Books · Maryknoll

Published by SCM Press Ltd, 9–17 St Albans Place, London N1
and by Orbis Books, Maryknoll, NY 10545

ISBN: 0 334 03054 4 (UK)
ISBN: 1 57075 227 3 (USA)

Typeset at The Spartan Press Ltd, Lymington, Hants
Printed by Biddles Ltd, Guildford and King's Lynn

Concilium Published February, April, June, October, December.

Contents

Introduction: They Can't Kill the Spirit

> Were I a non-Aryan or a not purely Aryan Christian I would be ashamed to belong to a church in which I could only listen but not speak.[1]

In his Apostolic Letter *Ordinatio sacerdatolis*, which was promulgated in May 1994, Pope John Paul II insists that the church has no authority to ordain wo/men to the priesthood. Moreover, he asserts that this teaching is grounded in the unbroken tradition of the church. On 18 November 1995 the Congregation of the Doctrine of Faith [CDF] published a reply or *Responsum* to the question whether the teaching presented in the Apostolic Letter is to be understood as belonging to the deposit of faith. The CDF's response does not raise the teaching of *Ordinatio sacerdotalis* to the level of an *ex-cathedra* promulgation but insists that the teaching is 'founded on the written word of God', and been 'from the beginning continually preserved and applied in the tradition of the Church' and has been 'set forth infallibly by the ordinary and universal Magisterium'. In the face of contrary results of theological scholarship and ecumenical practice, such an authoritarian rhetoric invites an investigation into the interests motivating this discourse of power.

Hence, the focus of this issue of *Concilium* is not the question of the ordination of wo/men but rather the non-ordination of wo/men and its impact on the self-understanding and practice of church. We are not interested so much in taking up once again the arguments for and against the ordination of wo/men as though wo/men were the problem. Rather we seek to explore the politics of power that has led to the most recent authoritarian assertions of Rome.

The issue at hand is no longer a 'woman's problem', the question goes to the very heart and integrity of church and theology. Hence this issue of *Concilium* focusses on questions such as: What kind of theological and ekklesial self-understanding comes to the fore in the prohibition of wo/men's ordination? How is the Roman discourse of power constituted and what is its motivating force? What is the social location of this categorical prohibition and what are its theological ramifications? Why does Rome resort to strategies of censure and repression instead of argument and persuasion? What are the fears that continue to motivate wo/men's exclusion from the sacred?

Is Roman Catholic self-understanding and ordained leadership inescapably defined in and through the second-class citizenship of wo/men? What makes it theologically acceptable to reason that wo/men cannot represent Christ, the Man? What makes it theologically admissible to argue that wo/men cannot be ordained because Jesus did not ordain wo/men although it is historically well documented that Jesus did not ordain anyone? What are the educational and institutional discourses which insist and guarantee that ordained ministry must be exclusively male? Why do bishops collaborate in silencing theologians and whole church communities who raise these questions? Is it the lack of faith that is always compelling the Grand Inquisitor to control or is it the fear of wo/men in power that motivates the men in the Vatican?

Why is it that the struggle for wo/men's full citizenship in the church provokes such misogyny? While working on this issue I saw a short notice in a Catholic newspaper that in a Catholic high school a girl had been chosen to perform the role of Jesus in the musical *Jesus Christ Superstar*. Because of right-wing pressures the principal vetoed her performance and insisted that a boy had to fill the role of Jesus. Her response was telling: 'I did not want to be a man,' she was quoted as saying, 'I just wanted to proclaim the gospel as Jesus did.'

This story reminded me of my visit with retired Cardinal Kim of Seoul several years ago. When I asked him how he is theologically able to defend the Roman politics of wo/men's exclusion from holy office, he told me that he had received a letter several months ago from a young girl asking him the same question. The letter was still unanswered, the Cardinal confessed. Whenever he tried to recount the Vatican's position he was not able to do so because he did not want to crush this young wo/man's faith and vocation. If there is no acceptable theological–pastoral response to a young wo/man's plea to serve the church and to preach the gospel, why then have bishops all around the world not taken a public stance against the Roman politics of power that is so destructive of the ekklesia?

Taking the questions of young wo/men seriously, the articles in this issue circle in different ways around the question of power and the theological self-understanding of the Roman church that comes to the fore in the authoritarian prohibition of wo/men's ordination. The first section explores the refusal to ordain wo/men. Hermann Häring opens the discussion with a very balanced ideology-critical investigation into the rhetorics of the Apostolic Letter *Ordinatio sacerdotalis*. He shows that the Roman position is theologically complex but consistent. The church is understood as a sacramental church, which is hierarchically structured, fixated on male gender and ordered in a monocratic fashion. This kyriocratic understanding of church is taught and reinforced as if it were infallible. As the following article by Acebo underscores with a quotation from Pius X: 'It is the duty of the herd to accept that it is ruled and it must submit to the injunctions of those who are ruling it.'

The second part of this issue of *Concilium* investigates the clash of ecclesiologies that comes to the fore in the problem of the non-ordination of wo/men. Leonardo Boff begins by tracing the vision of church as the people of God back to the Second Vatican Council. He is followed by Gregory Baum, who reflects theologically on power in the church and argues for a vital Spirit-impelled dialectic between three distinct teaching authorities: the authority of the hierarchy, the authority of theologians, and the authority of the people, authorities which are not parallel but intrinsically interrelated. Mary Condren approaches the question of power from a different direction. She argues that it is not accidental that wo/men are excluded from the sacred power mediated through ordination in churches that are shaped by the theological culture of sacrifice. Finally, my contribution suggests tongue in cheek that under different conditions one might be inclined to accept the argument of Rome that because of scripture and tradition the hierarchy has no authority to ordain women as priestesses or deaconesses. This argument would be believable if the Pope would elevate wo/men to the office of cardinal, an office that cannot resort to scripture and apostolic tradition for its legitimation. Of course, as long as bishops have to be male, all cardinals who elect the future pope should be female.

The argument in part three shifts from a critical investigation of the non-ordination of wo/men and the question of the politics of power to the ekklesial agency of wo/men. Melanie May not only tracks the global struggle over 'wo/men's place' in society and religion but also highlights wo/men's ecumenical practices for transformation. In a similar fashion Hedwig Meyer-Wilmes does not approach the question of ordination as a dogmatic topic but rather positions it within cultural-political debates on modernity and postmodernity. She points to the emerging variegated forms of church ministry and office in a postmodern church, which would be open for diverse strategies in order to engender wo/men's ekklesial leadership. Finally, Mary Hunt proclaims 'We Wo/men Are Church'. Rather than arguing for a modification of existing structures she details the different ways in which Roman Catholic wo/men claim their authority to create and shape new and exciting practices of ministry and theology.

The issue concludes with a critical analysis and documentation of the debates around the ordination of wo/men in former Czechoslovakia and with some concluding reflections of Hermann Häring elaborating five fruitful and encouraging aspects of new forms of ministry and ecclesiology that wo/men ministers and theologians offer as a gift to the whole church today. We end on such a positive note in order to encourage readers to claim their own spiritual authority as ekklesia and to continue the struggle for a more just church that is truly Catholic and able to appreciate the talents and spiritual gifts of all its citizens for creating communities and societies of justice. We are confident that if the next pope is elected by wo/men cardinals, s/he will find a way to shape ekklesial office in such a fashion that it represents the ministry of Jesus which was inclusive of wo/men and of all those marginal to the society and religious institutions of his day.

Elisabeth Schüssler Fiorenza
Hermann Häring

Note

1. Rudolf Bultmann as quoted by H. Jackson Forstman, 'A Chapter in Theological Resistance to Racism: Rudolf Bultmann and the Beginnings of the Third Reich', Douglas A. Night and Peter J. Paris, *Justice and the Holy Essays in Honor of Walter Harrelson*, Atlanta 1989, 268, who point out that already in 1933 Bultmann advocated the application of this principle to wo/men as well.

I · The Refusal to Ordain Women

Not Authorized by Jesus? An Analysis of the Roman Document

Hermann Häring

For many Catholics, the battle which Rome has sparked off in recent years has been one of the most remarkable and scandalous of battles. There is a history to it: as early as Pentecost 1994 John Paul II proclaimed that the church had no authority to bestow priestly ordination on women: all the faithful had definitively to accept this decision. After four years, we can add that with this statement Rome has started one of the most damnable and hopeless fights that the end of modernity has seen. In Western Europe, North and Latin America it has achieved the opposite of what it intended. Only now has the discussion which was meant to be silenced become vigorous; rarely have the waves of indignation risen so high. Never before has the opposition of theologians to a Roman decision been articulated so clearly, and never before have women theologians in the Catholic Church all over the world been shown so much male solidarity. The criticism has extended far into the conservative camp and has meanwhile also come to include the disapproval of many bishops. And it all began with an Apostolic Letter of not much more than one thousand words. It bore the misleading title Priestly Ordination (*Ordinatio sacerdotalis*): in strict Roman diction it should have been called 'The Non-Ordination of Women'. It was merely meant to remove some last doubts, but people had failed to see how great and insuperable doubt about the Roman position had become in the meantime.

How could such a serious error of judgment have come about? It would be too simple to cite exclusively psychological or power-political factors. Certainly they also play an important role; moreover the people who pull the theological strings in the Vatican are sufficiently well known. But I shall not be speculating here on the fantasies, wishes and anxieties of individual dignitaries. The question is too serious for us to personalize. However, from a formal perspective these dignitaries include distinguished theologians. They are not offering private ideas but represent a complex and in many respects consistent picture of the church and society. Again arguing formally, they refer to well-considered and coherent theological arguments. Their image of men and women, their interpretation of the Christian message and their idea of a well-ordered church all flow together into a single paradigm. For them this church ideally represents a church centred on the sacraments, with a hierarchical structure and a monocratic order, which in the name of Christ is governed by men. The scope and inner hardness of the Roman position on the ordination of women can be assessed only if we note the interplay of these different factors. In order to criticize this ideology I want to extract some perspectives from the above-mentioned document which clarify the theological seriousness of the situation. They relate to: I. The sacramental character of ordination; II. The symbolism of the traditional priesthood, which is fixated on gender; and III. The claim to an infallible decision. Here as a rule the argument is in terms of the 'tradition'. In the articles which follow in this issue there will be sufficient space for notions which take things further and shift boundaries.

I. Ordination as sacrament

1. A shift of accent with consequences
Without beating about the bush, in the very first sentence the document gets to the heart of the matter. As the first words say, it is about 'priestly ordination'. Largely taking up the official terminology of the church's *Code of Canon Law* (Canon 1008), ordination is described as the conferring of a ministry. It implies the right and obligation 'to teach the faithful, to sanctify and to govern'. Here the document is moving along traditional lines.[1] It is backed up by the documents of the Second Vatican Council and is open to many interpretations. So surely what is announcing itself here is nothing new. That is precisely the problem, for imperceptibly in its second statement the document already begins to shift the accent, and this will have an effect on the further argumentation. A comparison with the *Code of Canon Law* – which is itself above suspicion – can clarify this. Granted the new 1983 *Code* largely took over

the systematics of its predecessor (1917) in matters of ordination: the (sacramental?) 'ordination' to the church's ministries of bishop, priest and deacon is discussed as the sixth of the seven sacraments, as the first of the 'sacraments of status'. Therefore the phrase 'sacred' ordination sometimes occurs. But for the most part the texts of the *Code of Canon Law* do not use sacral terminology, just as already in the New Testament the sacral term 'priest' (= *hiereus*) has been avoided.[2] It is concretely about the legal enactment of an 'ordination' (i.e. acceptance into a 'corporation').[3] Alongside the more secular terms 'bishop' (= overseer) and 'deacon' (= servant), there is no mention of 'priest', but of 'presbyter' (= 'elder'). Granted, canon law on the ordination of women contains the notorious Canon 1024: 'Only a baptized male validly receives sacred ordination.' But precisely because no further justification is given for this shortest of all canons, its arbitrarily decisionistic assertion is manifest, and in the soberly functional context of the other paragraphs it is also open to attack. Finally there is a description of the general function of this tripartite ministry in a traditionally correct way with the triad of 'teaching', 'sanctifying' and 'leading'. Here teaching and leading are existentially demanding, but they are certainly not actions which can be understood in terms of the framework of the sacrament or the sacral. Why should women be less capable of this than men?

Of course Vatican II already set more sacral accents. For example, the bishop is 'invested with the fullness of the sacrament of orders' and is 'the steward of the grace of the supreme priesthood'[4] (*Lumen Gentium* 26); one of his main tasks is the celebration of the eucharist. Accordingly the priests also have a sacerdotal (= sacral priestly), i.e. strictly sacral, dignity. By virtue of priestly ordination (this too is a sacral context) they are ordained 'after the image of Christ, the supreme and eternal priest'. But despite all the sacralization, the Council texts also know other accents. As Leonardo Boff will show, the problem is that the Council could not decide between two visions of the church. Now in *Ordinatio sacerdotalis* – as already in its important predecessor *Inter insigniores* of 1976, which contained lengthy arguments – a clear decision has been made. Since the notion of the people of God is carefully being suppressed from the official side, the church (thus the Synod of Bishops in 1985) is now more and more exclusively being regarded as a 'mystery' and thus being one-sidedly sacralized. Following this reorientation, ordination, too is again being regarded from an aspect which has accrued to this ministry only over the centuries.[5] Now it could be objected that apart from the one term *Ordinatio sacerdotalis*, virtually nothing can be read about this in the most recent document. That is precisely the problem; for tacit presuppositions are also difficult to refute. The basic document *Inter insigniores* (more than twenty years old), to which Rome is now referring, was already clearer here. In it, above all in the fifth part, a sacramental argument and its consequences can be seen.

Of course we cannot differentiate here and go into the history of the concept of the sacrament at length.[6] It must be enough to point out that this document still presupposes a very traditional understanding of the sacrament, the differentiation of which has to be historical and above all exegetical. Four points might be recalled:

1. Otherwise than in scripture (which knows one baptism, one eucharist and the forgiveness of sins), seven defined sacraments are set side by side: the different perception and the extremely different significance of these seven rites are suppressed. In this way a more dynamic concept of the sacrament is suppressed by an essentialist one.

2. The statements about the sacraments are unhistorical: for the question of their legitimacy only a possible 'institution by Jesus Christ' is interesting and increasingly problematical. This has a particularly fatal impact on the Roman argumentation.

3. The central categories by which the efficacy of a sacrament are measured are (in narrowly legalistic terms) 'sacred authority' and its seamless ritual transference from person (!) to person (!). Persons stand in the centre instead of the question whether and how a sacrament can be 'a sign of the nearness of God'.[7] Legal questions and questions related to power conceal the theological perspectives, say that of the universal priesthood of believers or the end of all priesthood in Jesus Christ (Heb. 7–9).

4. If everything depends on a seamless transference of sacramental authority, then ordination takes on a central significance for all other sacraments, for only those who are ordained can or should administer such sacraments and hand on their own authority. These four points together give the Roman argumentation a monolithic style which levels everything down and hardly allows any differentiation of content.

Already at this point a general problem can be indicated: the theological discussion of this legally restricted concept of sacrament is largely abandoned on all four points. 'Sacrament' has meanwhile been recognized to be an unsuitable covering concept: institution by Jesus Christ at best still applies to baptism and eucharist; thinking in categories of power betrays hierarchical and not necessarily Christian interests; the fixation on ordination as a presupposition of the other sacraments distorts the original perspective of the New Testament. However, these objections are not yet noted in the argumentation of the passages concerned. The main problem of an appropriate critical discussion does not lie in the complexity of the problem but in the time-lag in the starting points. Here even I can only repeat old positions. In this way theology becomes a tiresome matter of being in the right: instructive dialogue is hardly possible any more.

Here it is neither necessary nor meaningful to deny the church's ministry of leadership any sacramental dimension. In fact this dimension governs the theory and practice of the ministries in the Orthodox, Catholic, Anglican and Old Catholic churches, as well as in other episcopal and presbyteral churches. But as we saw, even the language of Catholic canon law still indicates that this aspect cannot be the only one that counts. It may determine the perception, effect and religious category of such ministries, but it cannot become the basis for a definition of their essence. There are at least two reasons for that, which the document should not have neglected. First of all a commissioning to teach, sanctify and lead has a functional dimension: the qualities of catechesis, leadership of the community or diaconal services certainly cannot be derived from the criterion of a sacral initiation. Further, there is no dispute that the sacralization of the 'ministries' is not to be found at the beginning: evidently they were very practical and matter-of-fact activities. The initial openness, indeed absence of church structures, and the borrowings from the Jewish context and other contexts in Asia Minor speaks a clear language and for decades has been a commonplace in Catholic theology. Therefore no further analyses are necessary here.

2. In the light of the mystery of Christ?

However, the defenders of the documents mentioned will not accept this argument. They think it important that their concept of the sacrament has an indispensable depth dimension which cannot be discussed in functional contexts. For them the ministries of the church have directly to do with the experience and communication of salvation. Granted, this aspect is not discussed more closely in *Ordinatio sacerdotalis*, but *Inter insigniores* goes into it at length. The Catechism speaks a similar language. Both documents now describe the priesthood as a sacramental 'participation in the mystery of Christ'. Again each of the terms is loaded with traps. So I shall not discuss here some key problems which strongly shape the background of the document. Precisely what is understood by the *Mysterium Christi* or the mystery of the church? Are not institutions and legal definitions, up to and including the prerogatives of the papacy, over-hastily sacralized and thus removed from all criticism? Is not salvation again understood with an intensified one-sidedness in terms of the saving death of Christ instead of the coming kingdom? So does not the holder of the office again become the transmitter of the treasury of grace, which is then distributed in the sacraments?

We shall keep to the concept of the sacrament and the question why the Roman documents interpret the office of the priest in such a symbolic way.[8] According to *Inter insigniores* (no. 5), sacraments are grounded in 'natural signs', which are stamped on human psychology. We may follow this argument of a natural similarity (*naturali similitudine*, Thomas Aquinas). But it has been developed in respect of the classical seven sacraments. So the similarity and pictorial character lie in particular events and their symbolic power. Here in a very vivid way there is a washing away, a meal is held, sin is confessed, there is prayer and anointing with oil. Therefore against the background of such a definition it is not without danger now also to call persons and institutions 'sacrament'. What is meant is Christ and the church, as this has become established since the middle of the twentieth century.[9] For now 'mystery', 'participation' and 'sacrament' are drawn into the great obscurities and discussions in which talk of Jesus Christ, christology, has been involved for decades. Is talk of Jesus Christ about his cause of his person? Should we understand him 'from above' or 'from below', as 'God' or a 'brother'? Does redemption in Christ mean listening to his message, practical discipleship or an exclusively sacral act of reconciliation by virtue of his death? Do we get closer to his mystery by accepting the invitation of the original Jesus movement, or must we humbly submit ourselves to the divine nature of Christ?

It is quite clear that *Inter insigniores* opts firmly for the second possibility. The document presupposes a christology from above and accordingly a hierarchical picture of the church. A high theology of ministry follows: the sacramental sign is no longer related to central events (washing, eating, forgiving, anointing). It is no longer soberly measured by the (quality) of teaching, sanctifying or leading, but is personalized. Persons now become signs. Signs of what? This personalization of a concept of sacrament which was originally related to things has its consequences. In childhood, as the fruit of a pre-conciliar theology we sang the hymn 'A priestly heart is Jesus' heart'. Now again we can read, in a strange lack of differentiation, that the priest is a sign of Christ which must be perceived here and now (II 5). He is so to speak a living sacrament. This conception is confirmed by the Catechism: the fact that the priest is a sign of Christ, that he acts in place of (*in persona*) Christ, makes him indispensable for the transmission of salvation. This priesthood is 'one of the *means* (!) by which Christ unceasingly builds up and leads his church' (no. 1547). This is expressed even more crudely in a statement by Pius XII quoted in the Catechism: 'It is the same priest, Christ Jesus, whose sacred person his minister truly represents. Now the minister, by reason of the sacerdotal consecration which he has received, is truly made like to the high priest and possesses the authority to act in the power and place of the person of Christ himself (*virtute ac persona Christi*)' (no. 1548).[10]

It is almost moving, but we are also shown how ideologically misleading this concept is when the Catechism inserts an image whose almost blasphemous dimension I can mention only with protest: 'In the beautiful (!) expression of St Ignatius of Antioch, the bishop is *typos tou Patros*: he is like the living image of God the father (Trall. 3.1).'[11]

Against this background the decisive problem of the Roman argumentation is clear. The metaphor 'acting in the person of Christ' may still do for the celebration of the eucharist. One may say that in breaking the bread someone stands at the altar as representative of Jesus. But the metaphor may not be absolutized or personalized in any way. Anyone who represents the person of Christ *as person* (and not only in particular actions) in so crude a way and without any differentiation is even to some degree an image of the Father, he becomes not only unassailable but also master of any further action. He bestows salvation by acting. He can give a valid exposition of his authority by expounding himself. From an ideological perspective, one who holds office and is legitimated in such a way, who can virtually appear as Christ, is completely on his own. He *a priori* invalidates any criticism which comes from below (thus in terms of concrete tasks and functions, abuses and expectations, of oppression and situations of injustice). His office is made taboo and glorified, even if he personally feels it to be a burden and a task.

II. Ordination – a sacrament for men?

1. The appeal to Jesus

Those who are ordained, thus act in the person of Christ. The present-day curial theology reduces the question of church ministry to this high-handed and really also empty statement. The church ministry is stylized as a dignity which floats above all concrete conditions. Indeed one might say that this dignity is also made so universal that any baptized person can assume it. Certainly we are all unworthy of it, but by virtue of baptism we also all share in the universal priesthood.

That makes it all more the remarkable that arguments can still be found for the exclusion of women. Of course there is one argument which has the advantage of custom on its side: it is asserted that the church has never ordained women. So a historical argument which is developed at length in *Inter insigniores* and is repeated briefly in the more recent document is all the more amazing: Jesus himself, who was so intensely concerned for women, and who – in contrast to his Jewish environment – so emphasized their dignity and above all surrounded his mother with so much dignity and respect, Jesus in particular, did not call any woman to the body of the Twelve. If Jesus, who was so friendly towards women, did not do that, he must have been acting deliberately. Jesus did this 'completely freely and independently. He did it with the same freedom with which he emphasized the dignity and vocation of the woman in all his conduct, without going by the prevailing . . . customs' (no. 2). Both documents say that this attitude was simply confirmed by Paul and by the Acts of the Apostles: Paul by admonishing women to silence, the author of Acts by knowing only of an ordination of men in his reports.

This argument too has incurred largely unanimous criticism.[12] First of all there is the historical value of the statements. As exegetes are unanimous in emphasizing, the documents confuse that representative eschatological body of the Twelve with the later leaders of the community. Jesus, who appointed only men to the Twelve, simply did not 'ordain' any later church leaders, and had he ordained those first community leaders (say the apostles), this was certainly no sacrament in the classical sense of the word. Furthermore the statement in I Corinthians about women being silent (I Cor. 14.34) has nothing at all to do with the question of community leadership. And whereas Rome on the one hand clearly brings out the succession of the laying on of hands from man to man (Acts), it consistently suppresses the fact that in early Christianity there were women apostles (John 4.25; Rom. 16.7) and women leaders.[13] This procedure is simply dishonest, and therefore reprehensible, and after thirty years of informed awareness it can no longer be excused as negligence. But from the beginning the discussion has also indicated a deeper problem. Suppose we assume that – *per impossibile* – Jesus had ordained only men, what should we conclude from that? The press in particular already took this issue to absurd extremes in the reaction to *Inter insigniores*: if on the grounds given only men may be priests, must they then not also be married, perhaps be Aramaic-speaking Jews, perhaps be fishermen, perhaps be rather rough fellows with beards? Middle-class, highly educated and well-to-do gentlemen should certainly be excluded. And above all: Peter's successor would have to be married.

This argument and the amazing belief in its power of conviction disclose a prejudice and a purpose. The prejudice is that the burden of proof lies with those who argue for the right to ordain women, since the above mentioned Canon 1024 is *a priori* right. That is the only way in which one can make at least minimal sense of the strange argumentation. The intention is that the prohibition against ordination must be given simple and graphic support – with reference to Jesus. What could be easier than to be able to say: what Jesus did not do cannot be allowed today? Nevertheless, the argument remains unhistorical and quite arbitrary, at any rate for those for whom today this prohibition against ordination has lost all meaning and all plausibility. If one wants to argue 'historically' and thus anachronistically, the question is not what Jesus did then but what he would do today. Perhaps the friend of tax collectors and sinners (Matt. 11.19) would not adopt the venerable practice of sacred ordination at all.

2. *Representativeness as a gender category*

But here too a problem remains. Defenders of the Roman line do not understand this argument as a logically compelling proof. In this sense they claim the better hermeneutical awareness for themselves. It is a matter of disclosing meaning, in traditional theology called the 'argument of propriety'. Indeed *Ordinatio sacerdotalis* speaks only of 'grounds', of 'being appropriate', and refers to a comprehensive 'theological anthropology'. This cannot be analysed in more detail here.[14] But there is no disputing the fact that the different lines of argument in the curial position run together in this anthropology. Certainly one can draw positive conclusions from this anthropology. At a very early stage the pope – then still the philosopher Karol Wojtyla – developed a holistic picture of human beings.[15] He attempted to see human beings in their totality, especially as a unity of body and soul. Therefore already at an early stage he preferred phenomenological approaches in which human traits are described before being judged. As is then evident from *Mulieris dignitatem*, however, in a church context this anthropology becomes concentrated in a symbolic and symbolizing cosmos.[16] The pope has developed a strong sense of the meaning of symbols for religious identity. This can be misused. Not only do people live by symbols and for symbols, but the church too has developed a cosmos of 'supernatural' symbols in doctrine and the structure of its life, in which the cosmos of natural human symbols is now included. The relationship between God and creature, sin and forgiveness, human capacity and fulfilling grace is depicted along the line of church models.

That is probably the reason why being a representative of Christ, acting in the person of Christ, plays such a central and irrevocable role in his image of the priest. In this priesthood the symbolic dimension of human existence is now fulfilled. To represent Christ becomes the highest meaning possible with which human life can be filled. For what can be higher and more meaningful for human beings than the task of realizing God's concern for human beings, his goodness and loving-kindness, his love of justice and peace, his incarnate nearness to us as persons? There are strong humanitarian impulses in this anthology and it lends a sympathetic concern and warmth to many papal documents. But there is a sobering shift in the relationship between man and woman, an elitist male illusion, an unresolved opposition. The papal anthropology is so disappointing and therefore seems so scandalous because while it is so near to a reconciled and holistic anthropology, it fails at a decisive point. This is abundantly clear in *Mulieris dignitatem*: in the end there is no symbolism which unites all human beings, but – particularly in relationship to God – a contrary symbolism of man and woman. Whereas women symbolize receiving and receptivity, creatureliness and service, i.e. human beings as God's creatures (and thus include men), men – although like women they are only human beings – symbolize giving, creating, supernatural redemption, divine rule. According to this crucial theology, if I see things rightly, priests must be of male gender not because Jesus was in the most obvious sense a man, but because the Redeemer of humankind could really only be a man. This disregards the fact that:

- According to the Bible, human beings are 'created as man *and* woman'.
- The *human being* (and not man or woman) is said to be the image of God.
- The 'special priesthood' of those in the ordained ministry is unconditionally embedded in the 'universal priesthood of all believers' (thus including women).

- The gender-conditioned differences are not grounded in Jesus Christ but are definitively done away with in him (Gal. 3.28).

All this stands in deep contradiction to the idea of the holy power of men and shows up the proclamation of the dignity of women as an un-Christian and at the same time inhumane ideology. Dignity cannot be divided before God either.

This gender-related symbolism seems to me to be the decisive scandal in the Roman conception of ministry. Those who out of ignorance, cultural blindness or naivety prescribe discrimination against women can be taught better. Those who for reasons of church politics seek to guide coming developments and cultivate a good relationship with the Orthodox churches can be led to produce more sophisticated arguments or to adopt solutions which take things further. But those who consciously violate this most deeply Christian principle of equality between man and woman, those who keep women out of the sacral realm in awareness of the deep dimensions of religious symbolism, sin against the holy Spirit. Those who understand being a representative of God as a gender category have not even begun to overcome their own un-Christian androcentricity.

III. Irreformable and definitive

1. Recourse to the ultimate weapon

How serious Rome is about its male hierarchy, this 'kyriocracy' – which has symbolic and therefore also sacramental support – is evident from the last statement in the 1995 document. In 1976, *Inter insigniores* still ended with a conciliatory argument. A concern to overcome the oppositions was clearly expressed. The tone in the last sections of *Ordinatio sacerdotalis* is quite different and new. This is terse, and shifts from a substantive argument to a legalistic and authoritarian one, the clarity of which leaves nothing to be desired: the pope now sees himself as having the task of 'strengthening the brethren'. This terminology from Luke 22.32 refers to the passages about infallibility in the two Vatican Councils. The pope does not yet appear as infallible teacher, but the broad hint is clear enough. Now it is no longer brothers who are being strengthened but the rebellious who are being brought to heel. The pope sees no kind of authority for bestowing priestly ordination on women. Thus they remain excluded from the official ministries of teaching, administering the sacraments and leading the communities. All believers in the church must finally accept this decision. To exclude any doubt about its ultimate seriousness, Cardinal Ratzinger made things even clearer in a declaration of 28 October 1995: in the view of Rome this decision met the criteria of the ordinary infallible magisterium. Now after the Second Vatican Council the Roman magisterium has already approached the threshold of infallible doctrine several times: one might think of the encyclical on questions of birth control, *Humanae vitae* (1968), and the encyclicals on moral questions. But so far this claim has never been stated publicly.

First of all that prompts psychological inferences which do not exactly flatter the authorities in Rome, the pope and the prefect of the Congregation of Faith. They find discussions on this question a threat to identity within the church and to ecumenical relations. The developments in the Anglican Church threaten to break the dam; any ecumenical collaboration with the Orthodox Church is in danger. So the Catholic Church sees itself faced with the task of mediation in ecumenical discussion.

But these church-political considerations do not indicate the crux of the problem. For certain circles, the exclusion of women from the church's ministry is one of the core elements of church identity, above all its sacramental identity. They have no idea about processes of inculturation and socialization; change means decline. So they act unhistorically and apologetically with a touch of apocalyptic and in authoritarian style. Now it is finally time for the pope to play the last trump; after all he is the rock in the breakers (Matt. 16.18). So is the debate at an end? Church infallibility, too, feels under threat: slogans about holding out are proclaimed. Nevertheless, all the signs are that Rome has done itself no good here in the long term.

2. Immutable doctrine

Ratzinger's statement has not only provoked great indignation but also set off an interesting debate. The question for Catholic theology is: is this doctrine now infallible or not?[17] Here three levels need to be distinguished which are sometimes confused in the discussion: the levels of personal conviction (what is my view?), of a responsible institutional hermeneutics (how binding can and should statements of the church be?), and of the Roman position (what holds according to Roman rules?). No extended discussion on the first level of *personal conviction* is appropriate here. Those who follow the Roman argumentation on the ordination of women as a rule also regard the Roman position as immutably correct. But those who reject it because they think that the arguments presented are wrong, cannot regard it as infallible either. However, there is also a third group which regards this position as correct, precisely because it is presented as being infallible. This group can only be told that authoritarian arguments at most have a guiding but never a compelling function. In the end this group, too, cannot be released from the obligation to offer substantive argumentation and make their own judgment.

The level of a responsible *institutional hermeneutic* is more interesting. Even after the great debate on the infallibility of the magisterium at the beginning of the 1970s,[18] many Catholics remain undecided. Certainly they do not want any infallible decisions, but they do not reject the possibility of such decisions in principle. On the one hand the gift of infallibility is thought possible; on the other, infallible statements are bound up with such complex conditions that in the concrete instance time and again it is possible to wriggle out of them. Given such indecision, people readily overlook the fact that the theory of infallibility is always part of an institutional legalistic hermeneutics and was not aimed at a better understanding of the texts. The main question was therefore never: how are particular texts or contexts to be understood and how are they understood by the magisterium?, but: how and to what degree does the magisterium prove binding? The ideological confusion of all the theories of infallibility lies in the fact that – albeit with good intentions – they speak of the truth, but aim to establish relevant rules for language and action. So what is decisive at this moment is not the content of language, but linguistic action and its acceptance. Even if a good judge (the magisterium ultimately functions in this capacity) makes a well-founded decision, the basis for it can never completely catch up or even replace the decision, since communication and action remain different even in the pronouncement. This tension is also evident in *Ordinatio sacerdotalis*, which ends with an authoritative statement. To be brief, there is an argument in the first three sections, and a decree in the fourth; following this, further discussion is even prohibited. In other words, even the arguments presented do not function as arguments in an institutional hermeneutics, but only as the introduction to the institution's position. Many theologians do not perceive the harshness of such institutional hermeneutics, but confuse it with the hermeneutics of scholarly interpretation and the discovery of the truth. Catholic theology must finally ask itself whether and to what degree church action needs such institutional hermeneutics at all. The minimum demand would then be for doctrinal decisions to accept the conditions of true *communio*, in other words to have a democratic substructure. In no case can decisions into which the experience and the rights of half the believers cannot be integrated – as is the case here – be binding. That leads to another problem: under these conditions the possession of a binding character never excludes the possibility of revision, for the rules of action and speech for present-day Christians are always open to revision.

This leads to the third level, which is the self-interpretation of the church's, especially the *Roman magisterium*. At this point criticism and defence of Rome are almost indistinguishable. For in individual instances most of those who tolerate or defend Roman infallibility develop a tendency to strip a decision of its infallible character, while the critics tend to exclaim, 'Look, another unacceptable infallible decision!' How does this shift of fronts come about? In my view, in this debate it is often overlooked that according to official doctrine the magisterium, especially with its papal focus, has not only the competence to make binding pronouncements but also the right to decide on its own binding nature. According to conciliar decisions the issue is not only a binding force but an ultimate binding *nature*, i.e. the competence *of the competence*. This is comparable to the verdicts of the highest courts, against which no further arguments hold and against which no further appeal is possible, and to which they are therefore themselves bound for all time. We must see in all sobriety that Rome and the magisterium of all the bishops do not need to be told anything by women theologians in matters of the ordination of women. According to the official magisterial interpretation this document is self-explanatory, and the core of the arguments – pro or con – is no longer touched on. It is difficult to understand this absolutism; nevertheless it is still accepted by the majority of established Catholic theologians. This is particularly evident in the case of 'ordinary infallibility'. Certainly Ratzinger's declaration did not make *Ordinatio sacerdotalis* an infallible document; he could not have done that. He is simply pointing with the utmost clarity to the regulations on the ordinary magisterium which were passed by the Second Vatican Council. It follows that the prohibition and invalidity[19] of women's ordination are in substance infallible truth and thus need no further sanctions. The reason is very simple for Roman doctrine: the non-ordination of women has been and is presented by the majority of bishops, 'preserving the bond of unity and with Peter's successor', as an ultimately binding doctrine (cf. *Lumen Gentium* no. 25). Under these conditions, according to the text of the Council, 'in an infallible way the teaching of Christ' is proclaimed. For Rome the conditions could not be clearer. Neither defenders nor opponents of the privilege of infallibility could dispute this.

Now Rome had good reason for avoiding the provocative word 'infallible' for decades, although many regard it as infallible. The word was introduced into the debate at a moment when Rome felt particularly weak. We should not underestimate this weapon of the Roman magisterium for disciplining dissident women and men. The devastating effects on the occupation of professorial chairs, and on the nomination and regulation of women lecturers, is evident. But the *Ordinatio sacerdotalis* affair brings another problem to light: breakthroughs in Catholic theology cannot be achieved by isolated corrections. More than ever it has to be asked whether the church as a whole – including the marginalized among its members – is finally being taken seriously and accepted in the church's process of truth, i.e. in the sphere of conclusive argumentation and of binding linguistic action. The discussion on the non-ordination of women therefore also shows from this institutional side that today women not only can, but ultimately must, take up functions of leadership. The question is not only whether women may 'teach, sanctify and lead' but also when the kyriocratic halving of the church as it is will finally be broken. The church must in the end become the unconditional community of believers.

Translated by John Bowden

Notes

1. I shall not go into the precise terminology of the *Code of Canon Law* here. A *munus* ('office') in the strictly legal sense of the word can also be assumed by women. In canon law a rich palette of possibilities is mentioned, which I shall not be going into here. All these ministries are 'spiritual' ministries in the strict sense of the word; thus they are not official and strictly sacramental functions which presuppose ordination to the diaconate of the priesthood or sacramental consecration to the office of bishop and – according to current doctrine – need a sacramental authority (cf. L. Riedel-Spangenberger, 'Die Stellung der Frau in der Kirche', in P. Gordan [ed.], *Gott schuf den Menschen als Mann und Frau*, Graz 1989); for the legal system of ministry (or office) and authority, and the distinction between clergy and laity, see Knut Walf, *Einführung in das Kirchenrecht*, Zurich 1984, esp. 43–64, 169–88.

2. H. Haag, *Worauf es ankommt. Wollte Jeus seine Zeit-Stände-Kirche?*, Freiburg 1997.

3. Thus the *Cathechism of the Catholic Church*, London 1994, no. 1536.

4. *Lumen Gentium* no. 26.

5. A. Willems, 'Het Mysterie als ideologie. De bischoppensynode over het kerkbegrip', *Tijdschrift voor Theologie* 26, 1986, 157–71. For the process of consistent sacralization see already H. Küng, *Why Priests?*, London 1972 and E. Schillebeeckx, *Ministry*, London 1981; cf. also Haag, *Worauf es ankommt* (n. 2).

6. L. Lies, *Sakramententheologie. Eine personale Sicht*, Graz 1990.

7. T. Schneider, *Zeichen der Nähe Gottes. Grundriss der Sakramententheologie*, Mainz 1979.

8. W. Beinert, 'Dogmatische Überlegungen zum Thema Priestertum der Frau', in W. Gross (ed.), *Frauenordination. Stand der Diskussion in der katholische Kirche*, Munich 1988, 64–82, esp. 74–9.

9. Karl Rahner speaks of Christ as the sacramental 'primordial word' and of the church as the 'primordial sacrament'. Terms like 'root sacrament' and 'source sacrament' have also been coined.

10. This process of personalization seems to me to be more decisive than the 'Christomonism' which is often mentioned. The concentration on Jesus Christ leads to constraints only in the traditional 'christology from above', cf. J. Wohlmuth, 'Darstellung und Beurteilung der wichtigsten Inhalte und der Argumentationsstruktur der beiden Dokumente *Ordinatio sacerdotalis* (1994) und *Inter insigniores* (1976)', in E. Dassmann et al. (eds), *Projekttag Frauenordination*, Bonn 1997, 1–19.

11. *Catechism of the Catholic Church* (n. 3), no. 1549.

12. It is remarkable that the Papal Biblical Commission of 1976 did not come to the conclusion that the Congregation of Faith wanted, and among other things criticized the question as anachronistic. Thereupon the Congregation of Faith constructed its own arguments. This unworthy way of dealing with experts can also be noted in other cases: W. Gross, 'Bericht der Päpstlichen Bibelkommission, 1976', in id., (ed.), *Frauenordination* (n. 8), 25–31.

13. There is now a rich literature on the importance of women in the New Testament period. The works by G. Dautzenberg, M. Fander, L. Schottroff, H. Schlüngel-Straumann, E. Schüssler Fiorenza and K. Thraede are important. For a discussion of the exegetical (?) argument in *Inter insigniores* see L. and A. Swidler (eds), *Women Priests. A Catholic Commentary on the Vatican Declaration*, New York 1977.

14. For the anthropology of John Paul II see H. Häring, 'Kerk, wat zeg je van jezelf? De theologie van Johannes Paulus II', *Tijdschrift voor Theologie* 25, 1985, 229–49.

15. Karol Wojtyla, *Acting Person*, Dordrecht 1979 (translated from the Polish).

16. H. Häring, 'Het beeld van "de vrouw" in *Mulieris Dignitatem*', in C. Halkes et al. (ed.), *Boeiende Beelden. Feministischen christelijke visies op de mens als vrouw en man*, Nijmegen and Baarn 1992, 75–96.

17. P. Hünermann, 'Schwerwiegende Bedenken. Eine Analyse des Apostolischen Schreibens *Ordinatio sacerdotalis*', in Gross (ed.), *Frauenordination* (n. 8), 120–7.

18. H. Küng, *Infallible? An Inquiry*, London [2]1994.

19. In my view the term invalidity is suggested by expressions like 'the church does not have the authority' or more than a 'disciplinary significance'. Nevertheless this lack of validity, strictly speaking, cannot refer only to the sphere of the Catholic Church, since the Roman statement is at the same time described as a 'decision' (*Ordinatio sacerdotalis* no. 4).

The Silence of the Lambs

Isabel Gómez Acebo

> Our task is to lead the sheep to healthy pastures,
> free of the taint of any danger.
> (Pope Gregory XVI, *Mirari Vos*, 15 August 1832)

My title, borrowed from a famous recent book and film, is applied in this article to the church's practices of imposing silence on those who have dissented from its directives, since the metaphor of the flock to describe the totality of the church has been valid for centuries. Although the first image Christians have of the shepherd is of one who helps, who is even willing to lay down his life for his sheep, we should not forget that shepherds are also responsible for the health of their flock, which can mean sacrificing unhealthy animals to keep the rest free from infection. The problem in ecclesiastical history is that this problem has been perceived excessively frequently, with the weight of responsibility thrown on to the rulers, while the lambs are relegated to a passive collectivity with no leadership of their own. The above text from Gregory XVI is paradigmatic in this respect, though perhaps Pius X's words on the same lines are better known: 'The duty of the flock is to accept being governed and to carry out submissively the orders of those who rule it.'[1] In both texts the very possibility of the existence of voices differing from the official one is unthinkable.

The practice of silence in our church has become a common denominator in all its centuries of existence but has become more pronounced at times of greater uncertainty, in circumstances where the institution has had its back to the wall. It is well known that those who feel confident in their own authority have no need to have recourse to imposing their power, while it is lack of arguments that is made up for with dogmatism and imposition.

This is a serious problem, in that it tends to qualify anything that does not originate at the top as opposition and – even worse – as heterodoxy.

This can even lead to the conclusion that it is good for the church for numerous groups to leave it, since this ensures the purging of the flock and eliminates the weeds.

Behind this attitude lies denial of the right to differ, blindness to the fact that being different can enrich unity rather than threatening it. This blindness began when Roman particularism succeeded in displacing all other churches, demanding that they become Roman; when the Westernization of mission eliminated the specific features of other cultures; when conflicts could not be resolved and the followers of Christ split into various churches.

This prohibition of free speech does not make up the finest pages of church history, and if they are being dusted off here, it is in the hope that we may not fall into the temptation of using the same methods. The longing for a uniform Christendom in a globalized and varied world can lead to a desire to reimpose them. And yet the best way of resolving conflicts is by admitting differences when they are not fundamental, by talking, listening, and cultivating patience – an attitude that can provide the assurance that if pitfalls are avoided, the resultant society will be restructured on a higher plane of belonging and adhesion.

I. Ways and means of silencing

'Diotrephes, who likes to put himself first, does not acknowledge our authority. So if I come, I will call attention to what he is doing in spreading false charges against us. And not content with those charges, he refuses to welcome the friends, and even prevents those who want to do so and expels them from the church' (III John 9–11). This text shows that the problem arose in the early years of the church, since the authoritarian conduct of those who rule is a temptation into which most governors fall, even those who are well-intentioned.

Treatment of the voiceless

Those without power in society do not have to be reduced to silence: their words and actions are anyway disregarded as coming from those who cannot threaten the existing order; therefore, they simply do not exist. The church, though perhaps the institution that has done most to defend the weak, has also been party to this practice of ignoring those groups most disadvantaged by society. They are already passed over often in the Bible, as in the omission of any account of the possible callings of the women who followed Jesus of Nazareth. Even when these do make an appearance, there is a tendency to play down their significance. Hence the resistance to admit that Junia, called an apostle, can be a woman, or that gravestones of women bearing the inscription *presbytera* can belong to women who held positions of leadership in the early church.

Within the overall picture of neglect of the disadvantaged, one of the church's greatest failings is not lending its voice to slaves. It is true that several popes raised their voices in protest, such as Paul III in *Pastorale officium* of 1537, in which he threatened those who enslaved American Indians with excommunication, but despite this the Holy Office in 1866, in reply to a question, stated that 'it is not against the divine or the natural law to sell or exchange slaves, so Christians can do so with a clear conscience'.[2] Some years earlier, in 1858, the bishops of North America had declared in Baltimore, dealing with the same subject, that 'our clergy have abstained from any interference with the judgment of the faithful, which should be free in matters of politics and the moral order, within the limits set out by the teaching and law of Christ'. Were those limits not crystal clear with regard to slavery?

Even a canonized pope, St Pius V, was guilty of racism. The Papal States needed rowers for their galleys, a task so exhausting that it was reserved to criminals. When there were not enough of these the Rome police, on the pope's orders, rounded up any gypsies they found and sent them to the galleys: being gypsy was the same as being criminal. Many people of good faith signed a petition to the pontiff asking that these innocent people should be set free; Pius V responded immediately by having them all expelled from Rome, with the exception of St Philip Neri, whose huge popularity saved him. But the story has a happy ending in that Pope Pius was eventually persuaded by the dissidents and freed the gypsies before they reached the galleys.

The church has regularly complained about the restrictions other faiths have imposed on it in places where it is in a minority, forgetting that it too has failed to respect the voices and rights of others where it has been the majority. Thus the proposition that 'So the laws of many Catholic countries should be praised for allowing immigrants to practise their religion publicly' was condemned as 'error' in the *Syllabus* of Pius IX (DS 2978). Others, those who are different, such as gypsies, women and children, have no right to make their voices heard.

Besides having their voice silenced, women have been denied the possibility of choosing the way in which to live their Christianity. Only two ways were open to them: marriage or the convent. The most representative case was that of Mary Ward, who tried to institute a form of religious life without rules, habits or enclosure, governed by a general superior. Such a novelty led to a papal decree closing all her houses and throwing her into prison as a 'heretic, schismatic, and rebel against the Church'.[3] In her case it was not her voice that was silenced but her way of life.

Pressures

All those who venture criteria differing from the official ones can be sure to find themselves accused of bad faith, since they will be accused of lack of faithfulness to the papacy and even to Christ. 'Leave your conscience aside, Brother Martin; the only sure way is to submit to church authority' were the words Luther heard at the Diet of Worms in 1521.[4] The exhortation was repeated in 1832 by Gregory XVI in the encyclical *Mirari Vos*: 'That absurd and erroneous sentence or, rather, madness, which affirms and defends freedom of conscience at all costs and for all' (no. 6) – a freedom that Vatican II was finally to uphold without restrictions.

Meanwhile a series of practices was evolved in order to impute bad faith and achieve submission of the will of those concerned. A decretal of Innocent III[5] recommended denying medical care to sick people who refused the sacraments, even if this led to their death. Paul IV imprisoned Cardinal Morone for a presumed but never proven fault and forbade him to say or even attend Mass,[6] knowing how much this meant to him and hoping to extract a confession by this treatment. But the worst case of illegality and applying pressure must be that of Joan of Arc, who was persistently deceived by a 'friendly' priest sent to be with her, whose only aim was to gain her confidence in order to make use of her weaknesses at her trial.

Pressures are also applied to the world of non-Christians. 'We determine that, in every Christian province and at all times of the year, Jews of both sexes shall be publicly distinguished from other peoples by their mode of dress.'[7] The impossibility of going unnoticed, the intention that they should be ridiculed – a whole antisemitic posture not changed until, once again, the Second Vatican Council.

The weapons of excommunication and the Index

Excommunication is a measure applied to those who persist, involving total exclusion from communion with the church, which makes it the gravest of ecclesiastical sanctions. The so-called *latae sententiae* apply to situations in which excommunication is incurred automatically, whereas *ferendae sententiae* are handed down by a judge. Even in our time this sanction is widely used, and the list of those excommunicated is long and painful.

The sanction was notoriously applied at the end of the nineteenth century by the bishops of North America on those Catholics who remarried after being divorced. More recent is the case of Archbishop Marcel Lefebvre (d. 1991), finally excommunicated without a trial after being treated with kid gloves, according to many commentators, and certainly more leniently than his contemporary liberation theologians. Those who propose a papolatry or at least reinforce papal authority are better viewed than those who promote ecclesiologies of communion and greater lay participation, such as Leonardo Boff.

There are lesser degrees of excommunication, such as suspension and interdict, which claim to place persons at varying distance from the life of the community and the sacraments. The effects of such punishments should not be minimized: they can involve loss of academic honours and posts, but the punishment is mainly spiritual, since those excommunicated are barred from the sacraments. Today, the tendency is to presume self-exclusion from church communion on the part of the accused through not accepting set rules and postulates, since this clears the conscience of the 'shepherd', who is exempted from responsibility. This is a tricky time, when some maintain that the church has the right to set out its teaching without outside interference, while others see the questions they pose as fruits of the signs of the times and so as not to be cut off hide behind barricades of canons and *motu proprios*.

While excommunication places individuals outside the church, the Index of Forbidden Books placed many books beyond the reach of Catholics. This catalogue of publications was instigated by Paul IV in 1557and not suppressed till 1966, when it was seen that its existence was incompatible with the freedom of study and research decreed by Vatican II. The reason for its creation was based on the church's right to guard the purity of faith and practice, the right to obviate damage before it was done. This was a right extended to bishops in their dioceses and one that declared excommunication on all those who should read, print, write, translate, sell, keep, lend . . . any of the forbidden works. Sacred Scripture itself was placed on the Index in that it was forbidden to be annotated in vernacular editions unless these had been produced or authorized by the church.

Physical violence

When other pressures proved insufficient, the church did not hesitate to have recourse to physical violence to secure retractions. The operation of the Inquisition with its tortures, which condemned many people to death while the church prayed that their errors might be forgiven, is well known. The green light was given by the Lateran Council of 1215: 'Catholics who, taking up the standard of the Cross, prepare to exterminate heretics shall enjoy the same indulgences and the same holy privileges as are conceded to those who go to defend the Holy Places.' The mentality of the Crusades served to extend the same zeal to Christian nations and was the main prop for an open season on heretics.

It may be that some inquisitors acted in good faith, but I doubt their motivations in some cases. The Cathars, Waldensians, Beghards and others were movements that sought to return to the purity of the church's origins, strongest at times when the hierarchy was corrupt. Suspicions of the Béguines were based on their observing no rule, using the vernacular, and not being dependent on men in their unenclosed communities – a way of life similar to that later proposed by Mary Ward. This was too much freedom, so it was decreed in the document *Ad Nostrum* of the Council of Vienne in 1311 that 'their way of life should be permanently prohibited and totally excluded from the Church of God'.

The ravages of the Inquisition are too well known to need recording here, but as a woman I must just refer to the number of women burned for witchcraft between 1470 and 1700. They were mostly poor, uneducated widows, with no man to support them. The accusations of carnal intercourse with the devil are simply too fantastic to merit consideration and give the lie to the judgments made.[8] It seems to me that the sentences contained spurious elements of economic, political, or simply authoritarian interests.

Contempt for knowledge

For centuries knowledge was in the hands of the church, which did not hesitate to hand on the whole legacy of antiquity through copyists and amanuenses. This practice led it to generate a legitimate pride in its pioneering and leading role – which then came up against those who dared to dissent from its postulates. This was not in the theological field, but merely the result of other fields developing their own experts. One of the best known cases is of course that of Galileo, suspected of heresy for declaring that the earth moved round the sun. He hit the nail on the head when he wrote, in a letter to the Duchess of Tuscany in 1615: 'Theology should not stoop to the level of the humble speculations of the lower sciences. Therefore, its ministers and professors should not arrogate to themselves the right to decide on disciplines that they have neither studied nor practised.'9

Unfortunately, this learned man's counsels were not heeded, and the wrath of the church later fell on Darwin and his theory of the evolution of species, within a year of the publication of his book. It also, surprisingly, fell on vaccination, which was suppressed in the Papal States in 1815, along with that other dangerous novelty, street lighting. In 1829 Pope Leo XII felt obliged to declare that 'anyone who has recourse to vaccination ceases to be a child of God . . . Smallpox is a judgment from God . . . and vaccination a challenge hurled against heaven.'10

It was only to be expected that when biblical scientists tried to apply the methods of historical criticism to Sacred Scripture, Rome would raise objections, denying many of the postulates put forward by biblical scholars concerning authorship of the sacred books. In 1907 *Praestantia Scriptura* declared that 'all are obliged under duty of conscience to submit to the judgments of the Pontifical Biblical Commission . . . under pain of excommunication on those who contradict them'. As Lagrange pertinently commented: 'Today they are punishing me for things that will be studied tomorrow', as indeed proved to be the case.

The very essence of theology imposes on it an obligation to raise new questions, to rethink old ones, and to be open to new times; hierarchy, on the other hand, tends to become entrenched and to resist anything new that smacks of conflict. In the twentieth century the figure of the Jesuit Teilhard de Chardin is paradigmatic of this type of debate. He was first deprived of his professorship, and then his books were gradually suppressed. More outrageously still, he was forbidden to accept membership of the *Collège de France* and prevented from taking part in the international congress of palaeontologists held in New York in 1955. By the time he died in 1962 his works were known throughout the entire world, while the Holy Office published a decree exhorting 'all bishops and superiors of religious congregations and rectors of seminaries and universities effectively to protect souls (especially of the young) against the dangers of the works of Teilhard de Chardin and his followers'.11 More recently, the ban on the books of Fr Antony de Mello, like those of Teilhard diffused throughout the Christian world, follows the same line and is even more surprising in that his purpose is to amalgamate the message of Christ with cultures other than Western.

The ban on experts often goes with lack of consideration in personal treatment of them. Karl Rahner related that nine theologians of the German Doctrinal Commission met in Essen and wrote to fifty-two bishops, sending them his views on celibacy. Only two of them bothered to respond to the actual text; the attitude of the others was, according to Rahner himself, feudalist, discourteous, and paternalistic.[12]

Anonymous denunciation

Courts of justice require plaints against individuals to be made in person and will not allow anonymous representations; the same applies to the press in accepting letters to the editor. Most theologians silenced in the twentieth century complain that they have never known the origin of denunciations and have never been given the opportunity of a face-to-face discussion. In the nineteenth century Antonio Rosmini, the famous author of *The Five Wounds of the Church*, commented in his diary: 'All this work [of investigation of him] was completely hidden from me. And no reason whatsoever was given me for such prohibition. I sent my full submission'.[13] He is referring to the placing of his work on the Index.

Rahner complains with some bitterness that all prohibitions to publish were conveyed to him through the General of his Order without any written justification. With a certain irony he comments that 'such details of courtesy toward a poor friar were not, apparently, usual in the Rome of that time'.[14] In believe that if denunciations had to have a name attached, their number would be reduced in view of the problems in personal relationships that would then arise.

II. Dancing with wolves

The majority of these examples of silencing people date, thank God, from before Vatican II, when the church embarked on a re-reading of its essence and gave the laity a leading role. It is possible that there are inevitable cases where heterodoxy is obvious and clearly affects areas vital to faith. In such cases, with great sorrow and after the maximum possible deliberation, traumatic decisions may need to be taken, but such cases are likely to be a minority.

Today we live in a society characterized by such rapid development that the most modern discoveries quickly become obsolete. New problems require rapid responses, with the formulation of new hypotheses still to be proved. The challenge to the church is to evangelize this world, which involves – to borrow another recent film title – dancing with wolves, since the rate of change implies utilizing new means. The workers are few and their scarcity is increasing, since many have abandoned the flock. According to a classic work of political economy,[15] nervous people stay in institutions as long as they feel their voice will be heard, but when it is not, they depart silently, as the Maccabees did. They will flee from the town because they see no possibility of fulfilling the covenant there (see I Macc. 2.27–28). This flight is already a palpable reality in the church: workers, intellectuals, theologians, women . . . have left when they lost the hope of seeing their claims upheld. Our present task is to win them back.

The next problem is what to do with those who are left in the flock. There is a small group of saints for whom restrictions make no dent in their Christianity and, alongside them, a great body of people who have fallen into a 'death-dealing masochism'. I refer to another expert, this time in psychology,[16] who warns that people are disposed to relinquish some of their rights for the benefit of the common good, since this is to their benefit too, but, when excessive renunciation is required of them, they fall into this death-dealing masochism. They abrogate their responsibility, hand themselves over to superiors and fall in with the mass, which gives them the impression of power but in which no one asks them to take a leading role; these are the apathetic mass of the laity of which the hierarchy complains. There is no point in looking to them for the leaven and salt society needs so badly!

Machiavelli says that if one wants to keep hold of a city that is used to living in freedom, it is better to govern it with the support of its inhabitants (point 8). In the world of the twentieth century most citizens live under democratic regimes that have established systems through which people can make their voices heard, and a church closed off from lay participation is a scandal that keeps many away from the faith. I believe that the hierarchy should not suppress its rebels but listen to them, as they are usually the most creative spirits. It should try to live with them through an exercise of patience and mercy.

The fault, of course, does lie entirely with the rulers; there are those who try to force the pace of change without considering that the church is a very broad collectivity, in which not all can move at the pace of the fastest. This suggests that both pastors and flock should decide, jointly, to travel along a path of communion and brotherhood in the hope of creating a church that becomes better and more integrated day by day. In such a church, the prophetic word and mission cannot be lacking, since the gospel itself enjoins it: ' "Teacher, order your disciples to stop." He answered, "I tell you, if these were silent, the stones would shout out" ' (Luke 19.39–40).

Translated by Paul Burns

Notes

1. *Vehementer*, 1906.

2. Cited in J. I. González Faus, *La autoridad de la verdad*, Barcelona 1966, 123. Most of my quotations here are taken from this work.

3. María Pablo Romero, 'Una mujer de vanguardia: María Ward', in I. Gómez Acebo (ed.), *Mujeres que se atrevieron*, Bilbao 1998, 201–29.

4. H. Strohl, *Luther, sa vie et sa pensée*, Strasbourg 1953, 154.

5. No longer in the *Bullarium Romanum*.

6. L. Pastor, *History of the Popes from the End of the Middle Ages*, Vol. 14.

7. Fourth Lateran Council, canon 68.

8. See Caroline Merchant, *The Death of Nature. Women, Ecology and the Scientific Revolution*, New York 1980, 138 and 312.

9. F. Russo, *Galilée, aspects de sa vie et de son oeuvre*, Paris 1968, 331–59.

10. All in González Faus, *La auturidad de la verdad* (n. 2), 138. The words of Leo XII were reprinted in the review *Proyect* in 1968 in an article signed by Abel Jeanniere, on the occasion of the publication of *Humanae Vitae*.

11. *AAS*, 30 June 1962, 256.

12. *Libertad y manipulación*, Barcelona 1971 (Spanish trans. of *Freiheit und Manipulation in Gesellschaft*).

13. Cited in J. I. González Faus, *La libertad de la palabra en la Iglesia y en la teología*, Santander 1985, 64.

14. Ibid., 78.

15. Albert O. Hirschman, *Exit, Voice and Loyalty*, Cambridge, Mass. 1970.

16. Benno Rosenberg, *Masoquismo mortífero y masoquismo guardián de la vida*, Valencia 1995 (Spanish trans. of *Masochisme mortifère et masochisme gardien de la vie*, 1991).

II · A Clash of Ecclesiologies

The Uncompleted Vision of Vatican II: The Church – Hierarchy or People of God?

Leonardo Boff

The most detailed and careful historical researches[1] show unequivocally that:

   – Vatican II, especially in *Lumen Gentium*, presents a confrontation between two ecclesiological paradigms, that of church-society and that of church-community; there is undeniably a presence of a juridical ecclesiology alongside that of the ecclesiology of communion.

   – This confrontation represents two historical traditions, which divided the council fathers and still divide heart and minds in the church today, with no fruitful prospect of synthesis.

   – The first paradigm, historically, was church-community, prevailing in the first millennium; the second, church-society, has prevailed in the second.

   – The texts of the preparatory phase and of the first session of Vatican II are characterized by their affirmation of the church as a society.[2]

   – In the second session of the Council, the church-community paradigm emerged, and this was dominant at the time the whole schema of *Lumen Gentium* was revised.[3]

   – In the third and final session, however, the devotees of each model regrouped, and there was a sharp clash between the two paradigms. As no consensus was reached, a typically Catholic solution was employed: the maintenance of both, but juxtaposed. There was, as we shall see, a feeble attempt made to articulate the society and communion models in the term *communio hierarchica*.

   – In the course of the discussions two significant rearrangements were made, which were accepted in the final text of *Lumen Gentium* and which could point to a possible future synthesis. The first was the introduction of an initial chapter on the church as sacrament-mystery: this is an eminently theological vision, set in the context of a trinitarian, salvation-historical view of the kingdom of God. It seeks to move beyond, from the outset, the tensions between the two models in which the church has historically been embodied, and it affirms the permanent significance of the church as sign and instrument (= sacrament-mystery) of salvation. The second was the inversion in the order of two chapters: the second – the Hierarchical Structure of the Church, with Special Reference to the Episcopate – became the third, while the third – The People of God – became the second. This transposition is of major importance, since it gave priority to the People of God over the hierarchical structure. The function of the latter is then seen as service to the People of God. Furthermore, the term People of God gives the church a historical character, open-ended like a pilgrimage in time, in company with other peoples who are also journeying toward God, and it recovers the biblical dimension of the church in the perspective of alliance and mission.

So what is the relationship between the hierarchy and the People of God? This is where the tensions emerge, since we are dealing with two options between which it is difficult to find a convergence. In certain dominant sectors of the church these are posited as irreducible and a source of permanent conflict in both theory and practice.[4] If you read the category 'People of God' in the light of the category 'hierarchy', the novelty introduced by Vatican II is undone.

I believe a synthesis is possible, on the lines of Vatican II, but on condition of moving beyond a substantialist reading of power in the church. Let us examine the reasoning underlying both models and how they relate to the theme of the politics of power in the church.

I. The whole church, clergy and laity, is the People of God

The council fathers did well to place the reality of the People of God before the hierarchy. The term 'People of God' has the advantage of embracing all the faithful prior to making any internal distinction (between clergy and laity). *Lumen Gentium* links the common priesthood and the ministerial priesthood with the unique priesthood of Christ (10). While the baptized form the *messianic* People of God, all peoples, because they are under the bow in the clouds of divine grace, are in some way People of God (9, 13). To differing degrees, the People of God also subsists in non-Catholic Christians and in other world religions; even atheists of good will, who lead a righteous life, are not outside its sphere (16).

From this viewpoint, the People of God can be understood as the totality of all the justified, though in differing degrees of insertion in what we call 'church' (14–16). So one could say that redeemed humanity, receiving grace through living a just life, makes up the great People of God (5). In more systematic terms, based on Vatican II, we might say: humanity as a whole forms the People of God to the extent that it opens itself to divine visitation. The church in its historical institutionality would be the *sacrament* of the People of God and would also emerge as the *messianic* People of God.

Vatican II's whole conception of the People of God is shot through with the need for all the faithful to participate and commune in the prophetic, priestly and royal service of Christ (10–12), which is made manifest in active insertion into the various ecclesial services and in the charisms given for the common good (12). This People of God is embodied in the particular churches and the distinct cultures whose values and customs are taken into the church (13). Despite differences, all share equally in the dignity and common purpose of all the faithful in building up the Body of Christ.

The idea of the People of God sets the requirement for conscious participation, for community organization for a common purpose, for equality among all, for unity in difference and for communion of all with all and with God. As this is a People and not a mass, it has bodies entrusted with direction and leadership. But they arise from within the People of God; they are not above and outside but within and at the service of the People of God. A church in which, for example, lay people cannot share in sacred power, in which women are *a limine* excluded from it and cannot address the community, in which decisions are concentrated in the clerical body, cannot – actually and not metaphorically – call itself the People of God. It lacks the minimum participation, equality and communion without which the reality of People of God is replaced by that of an unformed mass of faithful who frequent centres of religious services and become individual consumers in a market of symbolic goods.

'People of God' will only be an accurate definition of the church and not a metaphor if it is the result of a network of communities in which the faithful participate, distribute responsibilities among themselves and live the reality of community.

II. The church as a society with a hierarchy of sacred power

The other paradigm of the church is found in the third chapter of *Lumen Gentium*, dealing with the hierarchy with special reference to the episcopate. Here another type of reflection is brought to bear on a body that is parallel or anterior to the People of God. The axis is not the community and the People of God but Christ and the hierarchy in a juridical sense. The category 'sacred power' (*sacra potestas*) determines this ecclesiological understanding, taking as its model the relationship a society has with its founder. Hence the basic paradigm is that of church-society. Christ, the founder of the church, transmits power to the Twelve, whose ministry is 'for the nurturing and constant growth of the People of God' (18) through teaching, governing and sanctifying (25–27). The apostolic college hands on the power it has received to its successors in an unbroken historical line. This sacred power is found in its fullness in the Pope united with the apostolic college and is distributed, like a cascade and hierarchically, to the bishops, presbyters and deacons. They all receive this sacred power through the sacrament of Orders, thus forming a special body (*corpus clericorum*) distinct from that other body, that of the laity (*corpus laicorum*) (the whole of Chapter IV).

This model of church is more one of a hierarchology than of an ecclesiology. The members of the hierarchy have everything, while the faithful, in terms of power, have nothing – just the right to receive. The hierarchy produces all religious values (on the level of word, sacrament, and direction) for the faithful to consume. It is a profoundly unequal, monarchical and pyramidal religious society. It prolongs the vision of Vatican I, centred on the supreme power of the Pope, now in Vatican II completed with a vision of the bishop who represents the Pope and the priest who, in his turn, represents the bishop (28).

Two aspects make this vision theologically problematic. Ministry is conceived within a substantialist ontology, and the ministerial priesthood differs 'in essence and not only in degree' from that of the common priesthood of the faithful (10b). The inequality is not just of function but of reality. The body of the church, in this view, is made up of two parties, which compromises the unity of the church. This is coherent with the view expressed by Pope Gregory XVI (1831–46): 'No one should be unaware that the church is an unequal society, in which God destined some to be rulers and some servants. The latter are the laity, the former are the clergy.'[6] The ecclesiological principles underlying this statement are found in their entirety in Chapter III of *Lumen Gentium*. Cardinal

Joseph Ratzinger pronounced on the same lines to the World Congress of Church Movements held in Rome from 27 to 29 May 1998: 'The institution of the church is based on the ordained ministry, which is the only binding permanent structure that constitutes it an institution; this ministry is first and foremost a sacrament, i.e., re-created ever anew by God.'[7]

Acceptance of this view poses a question: How does this tie in with the central affirmation in Chapter I of *Lumen Gentium* (4) and in the Decree on Ecumenism (2), according to which the church finds its supreme model and structuring principle in the unity of the Trinity, which is always the unity of three divine Persons who, while different, live in eternal equality of nature and communion? What is an error in trinitarian theology cannot be truth in ecclesiological theology. Any hierarchy and subordination in the Trinity is an error, yet hierarchy and subordination in the church are said to be not error but orthodoxy. This contradiction is theologically unsustainable.

This type of ecclesiology represents the ideology of those who hold power in the church. It is too contradictory to create communion and participation among all the faithful. In a perverse way, it legitimizes the marginalization of the laity and the exclusion of women. It represents a pathological state that needs to be cured by a vision closer to the utopia described by Jesus (see Matt. 23.8–12) and better founded theologically.

III. A broken bridge: hierarchical communion

The problem was seen by the council fathers. This is why Vatican II introduced the modifications we have looked at above, without, however, invalidating the society interpretation. But the conciliar texts make use of a term that might serve as a bridge between the society vision and the community vision: *communio*. Three levels of communion are envisaged: ecclesial (or spiritual) communion, which has to do with the ties linking all the baptized and all the particular churches; ecclesiastical communion, which is formed by the links between all the local churches and the Church of Rome; and finally, hierarchical communion, which means the structural and organic link binding all the members of the hierarchy to one another and all to the head, the Pope.

This last, hierarchical communion, is the decisive one, since, according to Gianfranco Ghirlanda, who has made an exhaustive study of the subject, 'it is the key to the interpretation of ecclesiology put forward by *Lumen Gentium*'.[8] The main reason for this resides in the fact that it is the hierarchy that creates the People of God by word and sacrament. Without the hierarchy there would be no People of God, no ecclesial community. Here it becomes clear that the hierarchy stands outside and above the People of God, since it is their originator and their leader.

The expression *communio hierarchica* was devised to be a bridge between the two types of ecclesiology. It took the *communio* category from the eccelsiology of the People of God and the *hierarchica* from juridical ecclesiology. The trouble is that the two terms do not blend. Communion cannot tolerate hierarchy: it is the name for equality, for the free circulation of life and of service among all. Hierarchy, understood substantialistically, as it is in this type of ecclesiology, introduces a break in communion, since it establishes an inequality. The only valid hierarchy is that of functions, since not everyone can do everything. Tasks and services are divided, but without breaking the basic unity in which all are equal and co-sharers within the community.

The expression *communio hierarchica* describes a broken bridge: it does not unite what it is suppose to unite – the People of God and a hierarchy of services and gifts.

IV. A coherent vision of the church as a community of persons, services and gifts

To build a bridge between People of God and hierarchy we need to start from the absolute minimum without which there can be no church. This minimum is the real and not metaphorical definition of the church as *communitas fidelium*. The church is not initially a priestly body that creates communities, but the community of those who respond in faith to the call of God in Jesus through his Spirit. The network of these communities forms the People of God, since the People of God stems from a community and participatory process. The various functions arise from within the bosom of the community. Some of these are permanent in character, such as the need to proclaim, to celebrate, to act in the world, to create cohesion and unity of the faithful and their services; then there arise services of a more institutional nature, because they respond to permanent needs better served by institutionalized functions; there are also functions that are more sporadic but equally important for the well-being of communities: charitable services, concern for the poor, promotion of rights and social justice, and the like. All types of charisma vitalize the community; they make it not only organized and disciplined but principally creative and productive of hope and joy, entities that belong to the gospel.

This ecclesiological understanding puts ministries back in their proper place. Their place is in the community, by the community, and for the community. The community makes up the foundational entity, and it is the permanent bearer of sacred power, the *exousia* of Jesus. Jesus did not see the Twelve as a hierarchy but as a messianic community. Inspired by the presence of the risen Christ and by the Spirit, all this community needed in order to function arose from within it. In it there is a diversity of functions, tasks and services, which Paul calls charisms or gifts (see I Cor. 12 and Rom. 12). Charism lies not in the ambit of the extraordinary but in that of the everyday in community. Every Christian is a charismatic in the sense that, within the community, each one has a proper place and function: 'Each has a particular gift from God, one having one kind and another a different kind' (I Cor. 7.7); 'to each is given the manifestation of the Spirit for the common good' (I Cor. 12.7). In the Christian community there is no idle member: 'individually we are members one of another' (Rom. 12.5).

Gifts constitute a structural principle in the church.[9] They are not something that can happen but also not happen. On the contrary, they are constitutive of the church, in such a way that a church without gifts (functions and services) does not exist. Hierarchy itself is a charismatic state. It is neither before the community nor above it, but within it and at its service. If all have their own gift, then we must also state that there is simultaneity of the most varied gifts. This diversity poses a basic question: Who guarantees the unity among them all and their ordering for the common good? So the need for the gift of directing arises. Paul speaks of this gift of assistance, of leadership, of having charge of the community, of caring for its unity (see I Cor. 12.28; I Thess. 5.12; I Tim. 5.17). The Pauline and Deutero-Pauline epistles speak of presbyters, bishops and deacons. The gift of unity has to be at the service of all gifts. It is one service among others, but with a special orientation as the bridge-element between the different functions of the community.

This is where the essence and meaning of the ministerial priesthood in its various degrees of hierarchical embodiment resides: in co-ordinating the gifts, in ordering them for a community purpose, in discovering existing but unrecognized gifts, in exhorting those who are perhaps putting the unity of the community at risk. In a word, its function is not the accumulation but the integration of gifts.[10]

Clearly, this understanding of church as community and People of

God does not exclude but includes the hierarchy. This is a permanent gift, a true charismatic state, because it responds to a permanent need of the community: unity among all.

Today the body of the church is split from top to bottom. If we do not seek a coherent vision that balances the relationships of power in the church, we run the risk that the Catholic Church we remain divided, which will cause enormous damage to the quality of Christian life. It is not impossible for it to split in two directions: on one side a church-People of God with egalitarian structures, participation, and communion among all its members; on the other, and in conflict with this, a church-hierarchical society, clerical, pyramidal and centralizing, which continually creates, reproduces and legitimizes inequalities, generating tensions and confrontations through its inability to adopt practical measures of participation in the church, measures that have become normal in secular society, and values dear to Jesus' vision, values of communion and equality among all as brothers and sisters.

In an ecclesiology of church-hierarchical society there is no salvation for women in terms of integration in the services and gifts of the community. They will always be marginalized, if not excluded. Such a fact is incompatible with even a minimally evangelical theology, which must incorporate human values because these are also divine values. This is the basic reason for abandoning an ecclesiology of society and hierarchy and building an ecclesiology of community and People of God.

Translated by Paul Burns

Notes

1. See A. Acerbi, *Due ecclesiologie. Ecclesiologia giuridica ed ecclesiologia di comunione nella Lumen Gentium*, Bologna 1975; H. Holstein, *Hiérarchie et Peuple de Dieu d'après Lumen Gentium*, Paris 1970; H. Pottmeyer, 'Continuità e innovazione nell'ecclesiologia del Vaticano II', in G. Alberigo (ed.), *L'ecclesiologia del Vaticano II: dinamismi e prospettive*, Bologna 1981, 71–95; A. Antón, 'Ecclesiologia post-conciliare: speranze, risultati e prospettive', in *Vaticano II: Bilancio e prospettive venticinque anni dopo, 1962–1987* (2 vols), Assisi 1987; L. Boff, *Die Kirche als Sacrament im Horizont der Welterfahrung in Anschluss an das II. Vatikanische Konzil*, Paderborn 1971.

2. See the texts and history in Acerbi, *Due ecclesiologie* (n. 1), 107–237; the texts in various phases of preparation and discussion are in G. Ghirlanda, *Hierarchica communio*, Rome 1980, 435–650.

3. Acerbi, *Due ecclesiologie* (n. 1), 239–437.

4. See the studies in *Vaticano II: Bilancio e prospettive* (n. 1); E. L. Doriga, *Jerarquía, Infalibilidad y Comunión intereclesial*, Barcelona 1973.

5. See the pertinent remarks by K. Rahner in 'People of God', in *Sacramentum Mundi*, Vol. 4, London and New York 1969, 400–2; L. Boff, 'Que significa teologicamente Povo de Deus e Igreja Popular', in *E a Igreja se fez povo*, Petrópolis 1986, 39–55.

6. Cited by M. Schmaus, *Der Glaube der Kirche*, Vol. 2, Munich 1970, 102.

7. Cited in *Adista*, 15 June 1998, 6.

8. See Ghirlanda, *Hierarchica Communio* (n. 2), 428.

9. See G. Hasenhüttl, *Charisma, Ordnungsprinzip der Kirche*, Freiburg 1969; W. Kasper, 'Die Kirche und ihr Amter', in *Glaube und Geschichte*, Mainz 1970, 355–70, also 371–87; H. Küng, 'The Charismatic Structure of the Church,' *Concilium* 4, 1 (April 1965), 23–33.

10. W. Kasper, 'Die Funktion des Priesters in der Kirche', in *Glaube und Geschichte*, Mainz 1970, 371–8.

Theological Reflections on Power in the Church

Gregory Baum

Present-Day Confusion

The contemporary period is not a good time for reflecting theologically on power in the Catholic Church. The Vatican's present effort to make the church into an ecclesiastical monarchy with dictatorial powers is unseemly and generates frustration on all levels of the church community. This effort consists of several strategies. Bishops are increasingly subjected to the control of the Vatican administration. Translations of liturgical texts and pastoral policies which bishops of a region have approved and adopted must be submitted to Rome and judged by Vatican officials who may have no pastoral experience in that region. At the Asian Synod held in Rome in 1998, many Asian bishops uttered the complaint that their pastoral guidelines and projects were controlled by Vatican officials who were not acquainted with the Asian cultures. Quite recently, a set of new rules significantly curtailed the power of the episcopal conferences that have played such a creative role after Vatican II. More than that, the individual bishops are excluded from their co-responsibility for the church as a whole, recognized by Vatican II as the principle of collegiality. The Vatican administration, often in the Pope's name, publishes judgments dealing with important moral and ecclesial issues without an antecedent discussion on these matters with the bishops of the church. The enforcement of unanimity in the episcopate goes so far as to demand that priests nominated for ordination to the episcopacy promise to agree with several papal propositions, among them the ban on the ordination of women, that are still debated in the Catholic Church. Against the teaching of

Vatican II, bishops are urged to think of themselves increasingly as local representatives of the Pope.

Related to the exercise of monarchy is the new Profession of Faith and Oath of Fidelity of 1989 to be taken by holders of ecclesiastical office and teachers at Catholic institutions. This profession contains the articles of the Nicene Creed to be held by faith, plus propositions of the Vatican magisterium to be accepted, not by faith, but by obedience. By confusing the levels of adherence, the Vatican tries to expand its power of control over Catholic thought. Since then the Vatican administration has intensified the censorship of theologians – without due process and without involving their bishops, often relying on denunciations sent by individuals. The purpose of the present witch hunt is to frighten theologians and catechists away from theological creativity and to conform their teaching to the Roman Catechism. Against the genius of the Catholic tradition, the church is becoming a monarchy.

Theologians deeply identified with the Catholic tradition have begun to criticize the bizarre situation of the last two decades when Rome has pursued goals and adopted policies at odds with the teaching and the spirit of Vatican Council II. Richard McBrien has argued that 'an absolutist mentality' has crept into the church after the definition of the pope's supreme and plenary power at Vatican I and that the present pope has adopted as his governing style 'the monarchical approach of the pre-Vatican II period, rather than the collaborative and collegial approach of Vatican II'.[1] In a parable depicting the church as 'a tribe', Nicholas Lash speaks of the present as a time when 'the chief elder of the tribe is a sick and aging man, a once most vigorous leader whose energy and single-mindedness are now contracting into obduracy. Around him, lesser chiefs jockey for position, hatch plots, and make alliances. Preoccupied with palace intrigues and the struggle for succession, their reaction to the deepening crisis in the world smacks not so much of leadership as of paranoia'.[2] Bernard Häring analysed the state of the Vatican bureaucracy in his Confession of Faith published in 1990 in *The Tablet*.

In the final decade of the second millennium, the collective paternalistic neurosis of a vociferous minority (at the Vatican) is getting worse. (These men,) plagued by obsession and fear, still live intellectually and emotionally with the old image of the Church as not just the possessor, but the sole possessor of all truths. The monopolistic mentality . . . is alive and well. As a result external relationships are being destroyed and, inevitably, neurotic internal relationships are being produced.

There is an atmosphere of mutual mistrust; the undercover world of informers is welcome; there is much striving for official recognition; and conformity is rewarded . . . Toward critical Catholics, (this minority) uses the sanctions of punishment and oaths of absolute loyalty to force the recognition of its monopoly rights in all questions whatever the faith and morals.[3]

An anarchist alternative

What I conclude from these observations is that the present is not a good time to reflect theologically on power in the church. In particular, Catholics who are affected by the restrictions of the ecclesiastical government experience power and authority in the church as an oppressive sacred force. Frustrations of this kind make the anarchist option seem attractive. According to anarchist theory, all power structures are oppressive and produce a culture that promotes injustice and inequality. Power structures distort the natural inclination of people to cooperate. The only hope for the renewal of society lies in the efforts of small communities at the base, which practise an alternative life style, engage in co-operative ventures, and in doing so foster the personal transformation of their members. Anarchist theory holds that people can live together in justice and friendship without a government ruling over them.

Since I have a good friend, a learned historian, who has strong anarchist leanings, I have begun to read anarchist texts, in particular the writings of Petr Kropotkin. This Russian philosopher offered a scientific demonstration that people could live peacefully in a society without a ruler. With other anarchists, he argued that governing power imposed from above wounded people's dignity, distorted their perspective and incited in them unnatural inclinations. Anarchists wanted no God, no king, no 'boss'. In his *Mutual Aid*,[4] Kropotkin argued against Darwin that what people inherit from their animal ancestors is not the struggle for survival, but, quite to the contrary, a natural inclination to co-operate. Mutual aid, he tried to demonstrate, characterizes the more developed mammals: it is for them – and for human beings – an essential condition of their survival. Humans are born into the world in total fragility, without fangs or claws, in need of agents that care for them. Kropotkin argued that humans have an instinct for mutual aid. They are by nature ethical beings with a sense of justice and an inclination towards magnanimity or self-sacrifice. What has corrupted human beings – the sin that tragically marks human history – is power imposed from above. Communitarian anarchists are convinced that society cannot be reformed or reconstructed from the top down by a revolution or a progressive government: society can only be transformed from the bottom up by people converted to mutual aid, living in alternative communities, and there recovering their natural virtues.

Christians have often been disappointed or even outraged by their ecclesiastical government because of its alliance with worldly powers, its will to increase its governing authority, or its blind defence of super-annuated customs and institutions. At those moments, they often had sympathy for the anarchist alternative. While the ideal of a human community without government may be an unrealistic expectation for the world, it may not be for the church, governed as it is by the Holy Spirit acting in the hearts of all its members. This was Tolstoy's reading of the Beatitudes. These Christians argue that the messianic community of Jesus Christ is obedient to a single voice, the divine Word, revealed in scripture and uttered inwardly in the faith experience of the disciples. In the church, they say, there is redemption, including the redemption from master–servant relationships: in the church we are all servants of one another.

The defence of truth

I am not persuaded by Kropotkin's secular argument that the human family can live in peace and justice without any government. While a small community may be able to realize this ideal, any major social project, however participatory, is in need of an acting centre empowered to supervise the widely distributed activities and make the daily decisions needed to implement the overall plan agreed upon by all. One cannot build a cathedral or an ocean liner without some sort of government, however dependent this government may be on the general will. The anarchist in our soul loves chamber music because there is harmony and cooperation without a conductor. Yet without a conductor large orches-tras would not make beautiful music. It seems to me quite wrong, therefore, to equate governing power with oppression or domination. Governing power is a good thing; needed even in participatory societies.

Nor am I persuaded by the application of Kropotkin's idea of freedom from government to the Christian church, guided though it be by the Holy Spirit speaking in the hearts of the faithful. There are two reasons, it seems to me, why the church needs an ecclesiastical government. First, since the church is not a small community but a major historical project, it is in need of an acting centre of supervision and co-ordination. Secondly, and more profoundly, the church is in need of an authority structure to protect the gospel which is threatened in the world: it is threatened because God's self-revelation is both 'transrational' and 'subversive'. The gospel transcends human intelligence and hence is ever challenged by reason in its various forms; and the gospel is subversive because it questions the dominant culture of injustice and inverts the standards of the sinful world. That is why the government in the church does not simply have an administrative function: it has religious authority. This is clearly testified in the New Testament.

Because the Holy Spirit, as the church's guide, speaks in the hearts of all the faithful, there exists an unpredictable logic in the interaction between those appointed to authority and the simple believers, i.e. between rulers and ruled. There have been moments when the church authority defended the teaching and practice of the gospel against the wishes of large sectors of the Christian people, and there have been times when reform movements among the Christian people defended evange-lical truth and urged the ecclesiastical authorities to wake up and listen to God's Spirit. There is a vital dialectic between the teaching authorities of the hierarchy, of theologians and of the people: these authorities are intrinsically interrelated and hence must be conceived as non-parallel. While this Spirit-impelled dialectic cannot be conceptually defined, it has revealed itself in the church's history, past and present.

Vatican II was an historical event in the Catholic church when pope and bishops were willing to learn from various reform movements that had existed in the church for some time, often under the frowns of ecclesiastical censors. At Vatican II, these reform movements were recognized as prophetic minorities, bearing a message for the church as a whole. Under their influence the church's official magisterium changed its mind in regard to the ecumenical movement (formerly repudiated, now seen as an instrument of the Spirit), religious liberty (formerly condemned, now strongly affirmed), the attitude towards the Jewish people (formerly 'perfidious Jews', now heirs with us of a common spiritual legacy), and conscientious objection to military service (for-merly rejected, now greatly honoured). Under the same influence, the official magisterium now promoted such innovative theological norms as collegiality, the prophetic mission of the laity, the right of dissenting Catholics to be heard, and the church's social mission to give witness to social justice and human rights.

Yet since Vatican Council II, papal power to teach and legislate has left its embeddedness in the collegial interaction with bishops, priests and people and is reaching out for monarchical control. At the same time, paradoxically, I am grateful for the existence in the Catholic church of a single voice of authority, capable of speaking out in the name of the gospel, such as Pope John Paul II has done on so many socio-ethical issues. He has supported the option for the poor, denounced neo-liberal capitalism, warned against the idolatry of the market, affirmed the priority of labour over capital, stood against dictatorship, condemned the Gulf War, sought justice for the Palestinians and received Arafat before he became respectable. Many of the pope's positions opposed government and public opinion in the USA, the world's single super-power. Several years ago, a friend of mine, an American theologian, said to me that he dreaded the idea that bishops were to be elected by the people. Why? Because he feared that the people would elect as bishops men like Reagan and Bush. In the unpredictable dialectic between the levels of authority in the church, the papacy today is a voice against world empire. One even wonders whether the pope's stubborn defence of the traditional role of women and the inherited code of sexual mores against the ethical sense of modern society is not due, in part at least, to the fact that the loudest protests against these come from the wealthiest and most powerful country in the world.

According to a structural principle implicit in Catholicism, centraliza-tion must be contained and balanced by decentralization. A clear recognition of the dynamic interaction between centralizing and decen-tralizing forces in the church is expressed in a recent statement (October 1998) submitted to the Canadian bishops by a group of Catholics, dealing with the growing shortage of priests, the increasing numbers of parishes without a pastor, and the physical and mental exhaustion suffered by the remaining clergy. The statement complains that the Canadian bishops have not commissioned a serious study of this issue nor have they examined the pastoral consequence of the refusal to ordain men and women according to new criteria of suitability. Here is the statement's plea: 'The bishops should no longer be restrained from undertaking the necessary changes for the benefit of the local Church on the pretext of obedience to the central power. It is not a question of encouraging insubordination, but rather of developing a style of action that encourages the taking of initiatives necessary to bring about necessary improvements.'

Sacred power

The church is not only a community of believers in which the divine Word is proclaimed and celebrated but also and at the same time the community with which Christ has identified himself. The church is marked by the principle of incarnation: it embodies Christ's redeeming presence in the world. The obvious manifestation of this are the liturgical gestures or sacraments through which Christ offers himself to his chosen people. The sacramental consecrations have introduced in the church the distinction between the sacred and the profane.

There exists a theological interpretation according to which the incarnation has overcome the distinction made in parts of the Old Testament between the sacred and the profane. The life of Jesus, truly God and truly human, is both sacred and profane, and God's self-communication revealed in Christ is offered in the ordinary situations of life where people express their faith, hope and love. This theological interpretation understands the liturgical sacraments as the solemn celebration of God's gracious presence in the whole of human life and hence minimizes the distinction between the sacred and the profane. Divine incarnation is here seen as revealing human life to be simultaneously profane and sacred.

Yet the dominant theological interpretation of the sacraments favours the strict distinction between the sacred and the profane in the church. The sacramental liturgy creates a sacred sphere in the church that is clearly distinct from the profane sphere of the laity. This sacred sphere includes both men and things. The men are the ordained, on different levels of sacred power; and the things include buildings, rituals, vestments, vessels, medals and other material objects. Traditional church buildings reveal the distinction between the sacred and the profane by the division between sanctuary and nave. To the sanctuary the laity has no access, a point emphasized in the middle ages by the rood screen.

As governing power in the church is always tempted to inflate itself, sacred power in the church is tempted to spread itself, i.e. attach itself to an ever wider range of activities, rules and objects, cover them with a nimbus of divinity, and exempt from a rational critique. A long time ago, I remember, the altar boys in the sacristy knew that the chalice was a sacred vessel they were strictly forbidden to touch; yet when the priests were absent, some altar boys, impelled by the spirit of transgression, would sneak up to the chalice, look around to be sure no priest was present, give the chalice a quick touch of the finger, and then withdraw in laughter and pleasure. The sacred creates taboos, and because of the exclusion it implies, it also provokes transgression.

From a theological perspective, sacred power is a problematic phenomenon. In their study of religion, sociologists and anthropologists have made the sacred a central category. The sacred, they tell us, is experienced as awe-inspiring, as manifesting higher power and as radically distinct from the profane. The sacred is said to ground the fundamental values of society and define people's collective identity. Emile Durkheim, one of the founders of sociological science, has argued that every society generates a set of sacred values that stabilizes its foundation, may not be questioned and summons people to become servants of the common good. The greater the inequality in society, the greater also the sacralization of the governing power. Kings and princes are enthroned in the context of divine liturgies. Following Durkheim's functional definition of religion, a good number of sociologists now interpret all institutions embodying a total ideology as religions. Seen from this perspective, Fascism and Communism have been called religions: they provided an authoritative interpretation of the world, celebrated their doctrine in ritual assemblies and sacralized their teaching and their leadership so that questioning them became taboo.

From a theological perspective, sacred power is an ambiguous phenomenon. Writing after the experience of Nazi domination, in his book *Die Macht*, published in 1952,[5] the German theologian Romano Guardini offered theological reflections on power. For him, power is marked by two characteristics: it manifests the capacity to act, and it expresses a personal will. Power is always the result of a decision. Guardini then makes a distinction between power (*Macht*) and force (*Kraft*), the latter producing effects in the world that are not based on personal will. According to this definition, thunderstorms and other natural phenomena represent force, not power. Their effects do not reveal a personal intention. While power can be benign or malevolent, force, from Guardini's point of view, is always dangerous. He laments that modern bureaucracies, due to their size, exercise not power, but force: they impose regulations in a mechanical manner without taking personal responsibility. Following this logic, 'sacred power' can deteriorate and become simply 'force', impersonal pressure, creating obligations and taboos, without revealing a higher care. The sacred and bureaucracy, one may gather, were the forces that made Nazi dictatorship succeed in Germany.

Theologically speaking, Guardini sees the model for human power in

God's power, manifest in creation and redemption. Human power, modelled on the divine, is meant to nourish, serve and enhance human life. Good governing is born of the Spirit: it presupposes the solidarity with a community, respects the dignity of its members, and serves their common good. Applying Guardini's principle to the sacramental liturgy and its celebrants suggests that the sacred in the church must always retain its reference to God's saving will. Sacraments mediate God's self-donation. Yet the sacred in the church could also become simply 'force' and be experienced as impersonal mana or magical efficacy. Guardini's theology of the liturgy, focussing on the encounter with Christ, freed the sacred rites from any magical elements. Guardini's idea of the sacred in the church allows us to warn the ecclesiastical guardians of the liturgy against expanding the reach of the sacred, turning it into an impersonal force, surrounding it with taboos, and attributing magical efficacy to it. As I have said, I remember the time when touching the chalice with unordained hands was a generally recognized taboo. So was criticizing a papal encyclical.

As there is in the church the temptation of 'creeping infallibility', so is there also the temptation of sacralizing ecclesiastical practices and institutions to protect them from being questioned.

Explaining the new cultural conditions created by modernity, Vatican II in *Gaudium et spes* recognizes that 'these new conditions have an impact on religion. A more critical ability to distinguish religion from a magical view of the world and from the superstitions that still circulate, purifies religion and exacts day by day a more personal and explicit adherence to faith. As a result many persons are achieving a more vivid sense of God.'[6]

Power in the church is both a necessity and a dimension of God's summoning forth of the community of believers. But this power has its limits – which it is often tempted to transgress. It is unfortunate that this important topic has not received the attention it deserves in the Catholic theological tradition.

Notes

1. *The Prairie Messenger*, 23 September 1998, 15.

2. From an article in *The Tablet*, 18 July 1998, quoted in *The Prairie Messenger*, 16 September 1998, 19.

3. Bernhard Häring's Confession of Faith was published in *The Tablet* of 28 July

and 4 August 1990 and reprinted in *The Prairie Messenger* of 17 September 1990 and, a second time, after the great moral theologian's death, in the summer of 1998.

4. Petr Kropotkin, *Mutual Aid: A Factor of Evolution*, Boston 1955.

5. Romano Guardini, *Die Macht*, Würzburg 1952.

6. *Gaudium et spes*, par. 7.

The Theology of Sacrifice and the Non-Ordination of Women

Mary Condren

> When he was at dinner in the house it happened that a number of tax collectors and sinners came to sit at the table with Jesus and his disciples. When the Pharisees saw this, they said to his disciples, 'Why does your master eat with tax collectors and sinners?' When he heard this he replied, 'It is not the healthy who need the doctor, but the sick. Go and learn the meaning of the words, *"What I want is mercy not sacrifice"*. And indeed I did not come to call the virtuous, but sinners' (Matthew 9.13).

As a woman born into the Roman Catholic tradition I entertained for many years the notion that I was called to priesthood. Together with many others I campaigned on behalf of this vocation, thinking it would only be a matter of time before the Vatican recognized its own logical inconsistencies, not to mention what it might have been missing by excluding women like myself.

The Vatican Declaration on the Question of the Admission of Women to the Ministerial Priesthood, issued in 1976, put an end to those notions. I had not expected that women would be admitted to ordination, but nothing in my theological education had prepared me for the sheer levels of what I considered to be theological dishonesty and the lengths to which the writers had been prepared to go to exclude women from the central rites of Roman Catholicism. As the prominent theologian Elisabeth Schüssler Fiorenza argued at the time, the Vatican was 'risking heresy' in its attempts to exclude women from ordination.

I realized then that it was not logic, but power, that was at stake, and that no amount of exegesis, historical analysis, or the most brilliant feminist theology, would make a difference. From that moment I set out to explore, not the explicit theological justifications given for the exclusion of women from ordination, but the deep-seated issues of power and authority; the mythologies, theologies and the underlying assumptions that undergirded their assumptions.

In particular, I asked, what is it about the logic, institutions and theologies of sacrifice that appear to be so inimical to the interests of women? In more recent years, my concern with sacrifice has developed with the aid of feminist theory, especially that of French feminism, destined to have profound effects on the way we do theology today.

Why mercy?

'I desire mercy, not sacrifice' was the consistent cry of the prophets against the petrified tired old logic of the reigning religious leaders in the time of the early Hebrews and of Jesus.[1] The Hebrew prophets uttered these words when the priestly religious leaders thought they could, through their efficient sacrificing, *control* the works or word of Yahweh. Jesus uttered these words when the Pharisees accused him of breaking the Sabbath to feed his disciples.[2]

Both Jesus and the prophets were saying that behind the formal observances that constitute religious life must lie a deeper logic, that of *mercy*, and that the logic of mercy transcends the immediate needs or exigencies of what churchmen might consider to be good religious order.[3]

The conflict between prophecy and order, prophets and priests is long-standing. In the history of Western religion, this dispute has been resolved at the expense of the prophets. Once respected members of religious structures, prophets are now only recognized and sanitized after their deaths by means of such institutions and practices as canonization. Notwithstanding the words of its founder, in Christianity sacrifice – its logic, practices, theology and political effects – and not mercy has been the dominant force pervading its theology, liturgical practice and ethical positions, shaping the very identity of the Christian churches. Disputes over who can and cannot perform sacrifice, and the theologies under-pinning such positions, were at the heart of the Reformations. Women in all those major denominations, whose theologies and liturgical practices are underpinned by sacrifice, are forbidden ordination.

It is no accident, therefore, that although major church battles have been fought over the issue of sacrifice, the question of *mercy* is left largely ignored. Sacrifice enjoys an uncritical status in religious and political discourse, a status that now needs to be fundamentally challenged if a theology of mercy is to be developed. In this article I will attempt to address the following questions: What is sacrifice? What are its practices? What are its effects? Why is it so inimical to mercy? What do we need to do if we are to obey the prophetic injunction and put *mercy* and not *sacrifice* at the heart of the theological and spiritual enterprise?

Defining sacrifice

One of the problems about sacrifice is the lack of any clear definition. St Augustine, one of the first to attempt to define sacrifice, defined true sacrifice as follows:

> Thus a true sacrifice is every work which is done that we may be united to God in holy fellowship, and which has a reference to that supreme good and end in which alone we can be truly blessed. For though made or offered by man, sacrifice is a divine thing, as those who called it sacrifice meant to indicate.[4]

In the critical notes to this edition of Augustine the word sacrifice is defined as 'a sacred action'. But this definition involves us in a circular process and begs the question of interpretation. As the theorist of religion, Roger Caillois, has said of the sacred:

> Basically, with regard to the sacred in general, the only thing that can be validly asserted is contained in the very definition of the term – that it is opposed to the profane. As soon as one attempts to specify the nature and conditions of this opposition, one comes up against serious obstacles.[5]

Nancy Jay, in her book *Throughout Your Generation Forever: Sacrifice, Religion, and Paternity*, provides a history of attempts to 'define' sacrifice (Chapter 8). But Jay ultimately concludes that:

> Constructing an objective criterion to identify 'sacrifice' invariantly across different traditions would be more distorting than it would be clarifying. To bring 'sacrifice' under our control as a perfectly defined object of analysis, to cut out and classify its constituent elements, is more like doing sacrifice than understanding it . . . The victim has indeed been brought under a kind of analytic control, but in the process it has indeed been killed.[6]

The interpretation of the phenomenon of 'sacrifice' or words such as 'sacred' or 'profane' is therefore no simple matter. The word 'sacrifice' is used by many writers as though it had a common reference or there was agreement as to the meaning. The apparent continuity of the word conceals radical changes in the intended content, and definitions of sacrifice are often circular, contextual, or self-serving. What is needed, therefore, is not a definite statement as to what sacrifice is in any kind of ontological sense, as much as a political exploration of the phenomenon. As Nancy Jay argues, a vital part of a sacrificial act is the post-sacrificial politics of interpretation.[7]

Happily, this coincides with one of the most fundamental tenets of feminist liberation theology: that it should be based on *praxis*, the union of theory and action. In other words, liberation theology asks not only about *definitions*, but also about *effects*. Or as the feminist theologian, Sheila Devaney, has argued: 'Not an ontology of truth, but a politics of truth is what is demanded today.'[8]

Indeed, the definition is intimately tied up with effects. Monica Sjöö and Barbara Mör expressed it very well when they wrote: 'We do not know if a god is a true or a false god until we see what kind of world has been created in that god's name.'[9] As we face a new millennium we have ample evidence of the *effects* of sacrificial theologies.

Happily, it is much easier to find out some of the things that sacrifice *does* than it is to find out what it *is*. Sacrifice *does* several things, and here it will only be possible to touch on the question. Sacrifice creates the other – demons or scapegoats; it sacralizes horror, it serves as a tool of social and religious control; it creates new origins; it resists self-awareness, the essence of mercy; and it attempts to *control* grace. Ultimately, sacrificial logic and practices represent attempts to limit, control, or otherwise jeopardize the work of Godself – the work of mercy.

Creating demons

An old Celtic text says that sacrifice is responsible for *rescuing the earth from the demons*.[10] In other words, the work of sacrifice is one of separation, the pure from the impure, the profane from the sacred. But who defines which is which, and according to what criteria? Are these predetermined or self-evident categories, or are there issues of power at stake?

While today we hardly talk about creating *demons*, the task of creating the *Other* goes on unabated: travellers, political refugees, homosexuals, blacks, or indeed anyone who represents difference – anyone who challenges the dominant status quo, as defined by those in power, become *Other* to the powerful religious or political establishment.

We not only *define* the other, we also *create* the other in order to assert our own moral, political or religious superiority. *Difference* is essential to this enterprise. Colonial powers, for instance, justified their colonial efforts to 'civilize' the natives by demonizing them, or their religious practices. For English colonizers, the Irish were often caricatured as monkeys, way down on the scale of human evolution, and hence in need of the salvation offered by English culture and civilization.

The theorist René Girard points out that it is not real difference that is threatening to the established order. What is much more threatening is difference that exposes the precariousness of identity. For instance, the pope seldom issues encyclicals against the ordination of monkeys. But the ordination of women is conceivable and women must, therefore, be kept at bay by regularly issuing injunctions, not only against ordination, but also against even *the discussion* of women's ordination.

Homosexuals challenge the precarious identity of heterosexuals. Men or women who are unsure about their masculinity or femininity are the ones most likely to persecute homosexuals. The most frightening difference, therefore, is that which is so close to the norm as to threaten its very being.

Foreigners, strangers, migrant refugees, all make ideal victims. Essentially, however, the victim serves to reinforce the boundaries of the dominant group. 'Fallen women', Magdalenes, serve to remind women of the awful fate that awaits them should they challenge or ignore the requirements of patriarchal marriage. Religious women, on the other hand, ideally serve to reinforce the norms and boundaries of the dominant group. Those who do not are very quickly suppressed.

In sacrificial logic, one's identity must be established *at someone else's expense.* Women and homosexuals are obvious targets, but the process of demonization takes place at many other levels whenever we are threatened by the possibility of change, losing status, privilege, or our place in the sacrificially created hierarchy.

Sacrificial logic leads to a perpetual state of war against the Other. As Nietzsche formulated the problem in relation to war: 'Ye say it is the good cause that halloweth every war? I say unto you: it is the good war that halloweth every cause.'[11] In other words, sacrificial logic *needs* constantly to create the *other* in order to assert its own superiority.

Politics of exclusion

The impetus to make *others* rests in some fundamental psychic and social processes, the full discussion of which is beyond us here. Suffice to say that the *other* usually represents some part of ourselves that we need to repudiate, vilify and reject as a condition of consciousness itself.

In Jungian terms, it is our *shadow*, the negative side of ourselves that nevertheless stays with us and haunts us as we go about our daily business. Having ostensibly repudiated it in ourselves, we recognize it in others and continue to persecute it there, lest it re-infect the purity of our social or psychic order. In sacrificial logic it is a simple matter to turn the *other* into an enemy: the one who must be kept at bay so that we can continue to believe in the myth of our own purity or goodness.

Once demons or *others* have been created, sacrifice acts to ensure that they are excluded from social or religious order. Those who disobey the laws, especially the laws governing sexual behaviour, are usually excluded from communion. They are defined as *sinners*; they are unworthy to participate in the rituals or partake of the sacrificial victim or whatever represents that victim, or to have access to the *fruits* of sacrifice, whether this be Holy Communion (in religious sacrifice) or political favours (in the case of political sacrifice).

Rites of purification, caste systems, represent pre-modern attempts to repudiate otherness. While these are overtly physical and dated, they have been replaced by their psychic equivalents that continue to run rampant. We persecute difference. We create ideal selves, ideal societies and ideal ethical systems that cannot allow of any difference.

Sacrificial theologies continue the work of sacrifice by dividing, separating and excommunicating (in the same breath as they communicate). Sacrificial theologies and philosophies are responsible for maintaining some of the most fundamental dualisms of Western culture, and for perpetuating 'sacrificial thinking'.[12]

At the heart of sacrificial rituals and theologies there is a scapegoat. Someone or some persons must be identified as having sinned. Once the sins of the community are projected on to that person, they can be cast out into the wilderness, leaving the community clean, pure and morally righteous. This very act forms the core of the community's identity. In other words, sacrificial rituals achieve the identity of a community at someone else's expense.

Sacrifice and gender

The work of sacrifice is the work of power: it is the work of excluding, rejecting and vilifying those uncomfortable parts of ourselves and projecting them on to a victim. Excluding the victim from the communities, we rest content in our own self-righteousness. The work of sacrifice is the work of war: the instant solutions of the politics of aggression, and the spurious power gained by demonizing the Other.

Although we cannot definitively *define* sacrifice, a primary factor in the ability of religions to effect relations of domination has been the mechanism of sacrifice, a gendered rite that, in the words of Thomas Aquinas, is an effective sign, one that 'causes what it signifies'.[13] Sacrificial rituals, in other words, are performative: that is to say, the medium is the message. The fact that women always end up on the wrong side of these divisions serves as our first clue.

Communion, according to sacrificial theology, is made possible by the sacrifice of Jesus. But communion carries as its converse excommunion, and the tool of excommunication has been used throughout Christian history to maintain church order, often at the expense of those whom the ministry of Jesus has specifically set out to include: outcasts, prostitutes, sinners, tax-collectors, or women-in-shame.

In addition, the exclusion of women from officiation ritually reiterates and reinforces their exclusion from other domains of religious or political practice. In most social and religious orders based on sacrifice, women are not allowed to perform sacrifice. Women are, therefore, the primordial scapegoats of the sacrificial order.

Notes

1. 'And if you had understood the meaning of the words: *What I want is mercy, not sacrifice*, you would not have condemned the blameless. For the Son of Man is master of the sabbath' (Matt. 12.1–8).

2. 'What am I to do with you, Ephraim? What am I to do with you, Judah? This love of yours is like a morning cloud, like the dew that quickly disappears. This is why I have torn them to pieces by the prophets, why I slaughtered them with the words from my mouth, since what I want is love, not sacrifice; knowledge of God, not holocausts' (Hos. 6.1–6).

3. 'When he was at dinner in the house it happened that a number of tax collectors and sinners came to sit at the table with Jesus and his disciples. When the Pharisees saw this, they said to his disciples, "Why does your master eat with tax collectors and sinners?" When he heard this he replied, "It is not the healthy who need the doctor,

but the sick. Go and learn the meaning of the words '*What I want is mercy; not sacrifice.*' And indeed I did not come to call the virtuous, but sinners''' (Matt. 9.13).

4. *Verum sacrificium est omne opus quo agitur ut sancta societate inhaereamus Deo, relatum scilicet ad illum finem boni quo veraciter beati esse possimus* (Augustine, *City of God*, X, 6; circa 410). Cf. Frances Young, *The Use of Sacrificial Ideas in Greek Christian Writers from the New Testament to John Chrysostom*, Philadelphia 1979. That this was one of the earliest definitions was suggested to Frances Young by Rev. Massey Shepherd (p. 7).

5. Roger Caillois, *Man and the Sacred* (1939), Illinois 21950, 13.

6. Nancy Jay, *Throughout Your Generations Forever: Sacrifice, Religion and Paternity*, Chicago 1992, xxv–vi.

7. Ibid., 10.

8. Sheila Greeve Devaney, 'Problems with Feminist Theory: Historicity and the Search for Sure Foundations', in *Embodied Love: Sensuality and Relationship as Feminist Values*, ed. Paula M. Coocy, Sharon A. Farmer and Mary Ellen Ross, San Francisco 1987, 84.

9. Monica Sjöö and Barbara Mör, *The Great Cosmic Mother: Rediscovering the Religion of the Earth*, San Francisco 1987, 393.

10. Cf. Alwyn and Brinley Rees, *Celtic Heritage: Ancient Tradition in Ireland and Wales*, London 1978, 79.

11. F. Nietzsche, *Thus Spake Zarathustra*, cited in Ernst Jones, 'War and Individual Psychology', in *Essays in Applied Psycho-Analysis*, Vol. 1 (1915), London 1951, 67.

12. Cf. Mary Condren, 'Women, Religion and Northern Ireland', Keynote Address to Women and Religion Conference, September 1992. University of Ulster, Jordanstown; Centre for Research on Women.

13. Thomas Aquinas, *Summa Theologica*, trans. by the Fathers of the English Dominican Province, London 1923, III, Q. 62–1.

The Emperor Has No Clothes: Democratic Ekklesial Self-Understanding and Kyriocratic Roman Authority

Elisabeth Schüssler Fiorenza

We are all familiar with the story of the emperor who paraded around without a shred of clothing. All bystanders pretended not to see. No one had the courage to tell the truth until a child in the assembled crowd cried out: 'The emperor has no clothes!' This story is an apt parable for interpreting the latest legal measures of the Vatican bureaucracy, which seems to be so desperate that it wants to enforce legally what it cannot reason theologically. Lacking arguments, the imperial government resorts to force. The means are familiar. They are the violent measures of silencing and exclusion. Facing the threat of religious violence, what is a feminist theologian to do? What should a good Catholic who is a feminist say?

I

Looking for guidance to Scripture I read:

> You are a chosen race, a royal priesthood, a holy nation. G*d's own people, in order that you may proclaim the mighty acts of G*d who called you out of darkness into G*d's marvellous light. Once you were not a people, but now you are G*d's people.
>
> (I Peter 2.9–10)

These words from I Peter have been not only the Magna Carta of the Protestant Reformation but also the guiding star of Vatican II. They affirm the radical equality and dignity of all the people of G*d.

We the people! We are the people of G*d. We are white and black, male and female, American, European, Asian, or Africa, young and old, able-bodied and differently abled, gay and straight, immigrants and natives. We are wise and foolish, theoretical and practical, courageous and timid, beautiful and not so beautiful, eloquent and taciturn, smart and clever, strong and weak. We are endowed with a variety of talents and gifts, experiences and hopes, faith and love. We are the image of G*d!

Every one of us is made in G*d's very own image. G*d who created people in the divine image has gifted and called every individual differently. The divine image is neither male nor female, white or black, rich or poor, but multicoloured and multi-gendered and more. We, the people, are G*d's visible representatives. Created in the divine image we are equal.

We are equal not only on grounds of creation but also on grounds of baptism. As those who are called and elect, holy in body and soul, gifted with the Spirit-Sophia, we represent Christ. In the words of I Peter, we 'are a chosen race, a royal priesthood, a holy nation, G*d's very own people'. These words are echoed by the Dogmatic Constitution on the Church of the Second Vatican Council:

> . . . those who are reborn in Christ . . . through the word of the living God, not from flesh but from water and the Holy Spirit, are finally established as a chosen race, a royal priesthood, a holy nation, a purchased people (*Lumen Gentium* 9).

As a purchased and freed people we are equal. As a pilgrim people we may fail again and again, but we continue the struggle to live and realize our calling to the discipleship of equals. As the discipleship of equals we are church, the ekklesia of wo/men.

To understand ekklesia as a discipleship of equals means to incarnate the vision and to realize the promise of the *basileia*, the commonweal, or, as Ada Maria Isasi Diaz calls it, the kindom of G*d. It means to articulate a vision of radical equality for creating a world of justice and well-being. It means to make real the vision of justice and love which Jesus, the prophet of Divine Wisdom, has proclaimed. As the daughters and sons of Divine Wisdom, we are made in her image. We are equal.

As her representatives we are ekklesia, the assembly of free adult citizens who have the right and duty to decide our own and our children's religious future. Ekklesia as the decision-making assembly of full citizens insists on the ancient Roman and mediaeval maxim: That which affects all should be determined by every one [or in Latin: *quod omnes tangit, ab omnibus judicetur.* Just so you feel at home reading Latin again!] In and through our struggles for change and liberation the vision of the ekklesia of G*d's life, giving and transforming power, becomes experiential reality in the midst of structural sin, of the death-dealing powers of oppression and dehumanization. As messengers and prophets of Divine Wisdom, the discipleship of equals is called to proclaim the good news of G*d's alternative world of justice and love. We do so by gathering around the eucharistic table, and by inviting everyone without exception to it. The ekklesia of wo/men as the discipleship of equals realizes this vision of G*d's renewed creation by feeding the hungry, welcoming the stranger, healing the sick, cherishing the earth, and being in solidarity with those who are oppressed by racism, nationalism, poverty, neo-colonialism and hetero-sexism.

It is ironic that in defence of the same Roman imperial structures which crucified Jesus, Rome continues to insist that the church is not a democratic community. Whereas in the last century Rome defended monarchy as the governmental form willed by G*d for society, in this century papal encyclicals have advocated human rights and democratic freedoms in society but insisted that these do not apply to the church. For instance Pope Leo XIII rejected all 'modern liberties', the freedom to worship, the separation of church and state, freedom of speech and the press, the liberty of teaching and the freedom of conscience, because the people were the 'untutored multitude'.[1] While Pope Leo recognized that there is true equality insofar as we are all children of God, he denied that there is any equality in society and culture. 'The inequality of rights and of power proceeds from the very Author of nature, "from whom all paternity in heaven and earth" is named.'[2] The pope pointed out that 'the abilities of all are not equal, as one differs from another in the powers of mind or body, and there are much dissimilarity of manner, disposition and character'. Hence, he argues, 'it is most repugnant to reason to endeavour to confine all within the same measure and to extend complete equality to the institutions of civil life'.[3] Here difference is not understood as giftedness but construed as inequality in kyriarchal terms (domination of Lord/Master/Father/Husband).

Although the word ekklesia is usually translated in English as 'church', the English word 'church' derives from the Greek word 'kyriake' i.e.

belonging to the lord/master/father and not from the Greek term 'ekklesia'. The translation process which has transformed 'ekklesia/ congress' into 'kyriake/church' indicates a historical development that has privileged the kyriarchal, Roman imperial form of church. This 'church' is characterized by hierarchical structures, represented by men, and divided into a sacred two-class system of the ordained and the laity. Hence the expression laity/lay is not derived from the Greek *laos* = the people but from *laikos*, which characterizes someone as a subordinate of the clergy. It means those who are uneducated and belong to the 'secular' realm, those who have no power and status in the church. Because of their gender wo/men are always laity. 'Laywo/man' is a pejorative and derogatory term connoting second-class citizenship.

Equality is often construed in the sense in which Pope Leo XIII understood it. It is defined as sameness rather than as equal standing. According to the common-sense notion of equality, for wo/men to become equal means that they have to become like men, just as for blacks to become equal means they have to become like whites, or for the laity to become equal they have to become like clergymen. On this view maleness, whiteness and clergy status are the standards not only for ordination but also for being human and Christian. As long as structures of domination and subordination exist, equality is possible only for those who hold kyriarchal power. This is the reason why Rome insists that it cannot ordain wo/men.

But equality can also mean status equivalence, equitability and parity on grounds of having diverse gifts and experiences. Diversity and differences do not diminish equality but enhance it. In this under-standing equality is closely aligned with justice. In a radical democratic vision of church, equality means equal access, equal respect, equal rights and equal well-being. It must be realized as political, economic, social, cultural, religious, ekklesial equality. It does not spell sameness but difference and heterogeneity, inclusivity and partnership, self-determi-nation and alternating leadership rooted in different gifts and capabil-ities.

In the past decades Catholic wo/men have taken the vision of church as the discipleship of equals very seriously. We have consistently main-tained that we must be acknowledged as human and ekklesial subjects with equal rights and dignity rather than remain objects of kyriarchal theology and clerical governance. Nevertheless our call to conversion from ecclesiastical and societal kyriarchy has generally been met with outright rejection or subtle co-optation. We have denounced the structural and personal sin of kyriarchal sexism and have claimed our ekklesial dignity, rights and responsibilities. Yet those who advocate kyriarchal restoration of church and theology continue to insist either on wo/men's exclusion from decision-making powers in the church or on our conformity with traditional hierarchical teachings. The church understood as clerical-patriarchal hierarchy not only is exclusive of wo/men in ordained leadership, but also requires a kyriocentric symbol system for its legitimation. Jesus' insistence that structures of domination should not be tolerated in the discipleship of equals is forgotten. Rather, those who 'would be' great or first among the disciples must be slaves and servants of all (Mark 9.33–37; 10.42–45; Matt. 20.26–27; Luke 22.24–27). This Jesus-tradition is blatantly violated by *Ad Tuendam Fidei*, whereas a non-existing Jesus-tradition prohibiting the ordination of wo/men is invoked and enforced. Indeed, the emperor has no clothes!

II

It seems that summers (and not just summers) are a dangerous time for wo/men in the Roman Catholic Church, especially for those of us who are feminists and/or theologians. One wonders whether there is an anti-wo/man virus abroad affecting the mental health of some Vatican prelates, a virus that seems to become virulent during the summer months. Maybe it is the Roman heat? Or maybe it is the El Nino effect that causes such malaise?

Five years ago, in May 1994, a papal Apostolic Letter *Ordinatio sacerdotalis* arrived, stating that the church has no authority whatever to confer priestly ordination on wo/men. Yet many Christian churches that are reading the same scriptures have claimed the authority to ordain wo/men. Who is the church that has 'no authority'? Is it only the Roman church or the Pope and the Curia? It must be the fever caused by the anti-wo/man virus that has such strange effects, which reduce the church that has 'no authority' to a limited number of [old] celibate men. Don't get me wrong! I love men, but I love the church too.

At the end of June 1998 a new missive has made its way to the press trying to reach the faithful with legal intimidation. Under threat of heavy censure and punishment the latest *motu proprio Ad Tuendam Fidem* seeks to eliminate the remnants of 'the lawful freedom of inquiry and of thought and the freedom to express it' which the Pastoral Constitution of Vatican II on *The Church in the Modern World* had promised. The prohibition of euthanasia and prostitution, as well as the exclusion of women from ordination, are the examples which are given in the commentary of the Congregation of the Doctrine of Faith (CDF) for the authoritative teachings that may not be questioned. It is obvious that this most recent papal decree attempts to silence once and for all women's claim to full ekklesial citizenship. Hence the language of the document is more Roman imperial than evangelical-conciliar. Its legalistic measures bespeak the fear of Dostoievsky's Grand Inquisitor:

> In order to safeguard the faith of the Catholic Church against errors springing up among certain of Christ's faithful, especially among those who apply themselves as scholars to the study of sacred theology, it has seemed most necessary to Us, whose chief duty is to confirm Our brothers (sic) in the faith (cf. Luke 22.32), that certain norms should be added to the texts of the Code of Canon Law and of the Code of Canons of the Eastern Churches currently in force, by means of which the duty of upholding the truth definitely proposed by the Church's Magisterium may be expressly imposed and canonical sanctions related to this duty also noted.

Those who disagree are to be warned and then punished as heretics or apostates by excommunication or another appropriate and just penalty.

On Thursday, 10 September 1998, the Australian military bishop, Bishop Geoffrey Mayne, who is also parish priest of St Thomas More's Parish, Campbell, a suburb of Canberra in the Australian Capital Territory, advised the Ordination of Catholic Women national executive member, Ann Nugent, that she would not be given communion by him or by his assistant priest, Monsignor Fuller. He said he was acting as her parish priest and in accord with the Pope's apostolic letter (*Ad Tuendarn Fidem*) and Cardinal Ratzinger's commentary. Not satisfied at being given these instructions by phone, Ann arranged an interview with the Bishop at his chancellery on Tuesday, 15 September. At this meeting the Bishop reaffirmed the directions he had given that Ann was not:
* to receive communion at St Thomas More's parish church;
* to continue as a member of St Thomas More's Parish Pastoral Council;
* to continue on the reading roster at St Thomas More's.[4]

The language of the Inquisition threatening penalization and expulsion from the church that was rejected by the Second Vatican Council is at work again here. While the Holy Father apologizes for the killing of witches several hundred years ago, the Roman gerontocracy uses the same measures of silencing and exclusion against wo/men today. Luckily, Vatican State no longer has the power to burn us as witches and heretics at the stake! We must not forget, however, that the authorities have only as much power and authority as we, the faithful, grant them. Nevertheless, I fear that this coming summer the virus could do ever greater harm to the ekklesia.

After having made the diagnosis, what does the doctor prescribe in such a situation? Let's treat this Roman malaise like a common cold, she advises. Just as according to common wisdom a summer cold lasts when treated with medicine a week and when left alone seven days, so this will pass. The best medicine against it is to leave it alone. Besides, *Ad Tuendam Fidem* does not speak to wo/men. As far as I can see it is only addressed to the 'brothers'. Androcentric language has its advantages! Remember the wisdom of our nineteenth-century foremothers: No taxation without representation! In this century Virginia Woolf tells us that we must 'kill the Angel in the house', the good girl voice that for ever urges us to please.

So what is a good Catholic girl to do? I suggest that those of us who are called to priestly ministry continue to act on this call, celebrating the eucharist, serving the poor, teaching the young, and building up the ekklesia. If they want to join the clergy, there are plenty of churches that will welcome them with open arms. However, those of us who are called to leadership for the renewal of the Catholic church must take the Holy Father at his word when he says that he does not have the authority to ordain wo/men at priests. Granted this is the case, we ask, what about cardinals?

The office of cardinal was instituted to provide a court for the pope. Hence cardinals are called the princes of the church! No ordination is required for this important office either by scripture or tradition. Moreover, there is no evidence that the office of cardinal goes back either to Jesus or to the apostles. True, it has a long malestream tradition, but this tradition is of the hierarchy's making. Hence the Holy Father is free to appoint the first wo/men cardinal in the next couple of weeks after the summer virus has subsided. *If Commonweal* is correct that Pope John Paul II has declared himself to be a '*papa feminista*', the first wo/man to be cardinal will be a feminist!

As I have suggested a long time ago, those fighting for the ordination of wo/men ought to organize for achieving the goal of cardinalship. The demand to become cardinals does not generate scriptural manipulation nor engender the christological heresy of androcentrism as distinct from the politics of power that prohibits the discussion of wo/men's priestly ordination and must resort of ideological legitimation. Hence the appointment of wo/men as cardinals would be the best medicine to cure the Roman malaise. The election and appointment of wo/men as cardinals would get rid of the misogynist virus that afflicts our church and leads to its paralysis. It also would open up to wo/men democratic means to determine the papacy and thereby the future of the church.

Needless to say, equity would demand that all cardinals should be wo/men, as long as bishops must remain men. Let's obey the papal decree and declare a moratorium on demands for the ordination of wo/men as deaconesses or priestesses. Instead let us get ready for the next Consistorium when wo/men cardinals will elect the new successor of Peter or – as I would have it – the successor of Mary of Magdala!

Maybe the new pope will be one of us! If she can't symbolize Christ as his Vicar, I am sure she could very convincingly represent Mother Church. I would love to serve her as head of the CDF [the acronym for the Latin *Congregatio Doctorum Feminisatrum*]. Until then, I recommend that we tell again and again the story of the Emperor who has no clothes as an imaginative antidote against the Roman summer cold.

Notes

1. Charles E. Curran, 'What Catholic Ecclesiology Can Learn from Official Catholic Social Teaching', 105.

2. Pope Leo XIII, 'On Socialism', in E. Gilson (ed.), *The Church Speaks to the Modern World: The Social Teachings of Leo XIII*, Garden City, NY 1954, 193.

3. Pope Leo XIII, 'On Freemasonry', in ibid., 130.

4. Ordination of Catholic Women Incorporated, PO Box E418, Kingston, ACT 2604, Australia.

III · Practices for Transformation

The Diversity of Ministries in a Postmodern Church[1]

Hedwig Meyer-Wilmes

Our Western European culture is characterized by a unique gulf. On the one hand interest in religious institutions is steadily declining, while on the other there is a growing need for religion in the lives of individuals. That is expressed, for example, in the decline of churchgoing and the large numbers of people leaving the two great confessions in Germany alongside the simultaneous increase in those attending church conferences, both Catholic and Protestant. The church, too, seems to be involved in the trend. The diagnosis of this situation is that of an increasing individualization and secularization of society, and this diagnosis is presented sometimes with sorrow, sometimes polemically. Secularization is understood as the increasing lack of religion in society, and individualization is understood as a detachment from traditional forms of life in favour of a self-centredness which is felt to be emancipation.

That means that individualization becomes a leading concept in a pessimistic interpretation of culture, and secularization the basis of the 'emigration of the church from society'.[2] In such a view the church becomes a last bastion of a sense of community and tradition. The church is seen over against society as an institution which is not itself subject to the influences of modern society. 'To establish the identity of the church we first ascertain the social context in which it exists, that of secularization. This context helps to determine the identity of the church, but the church is not just determined by it.'[3] That means that the church is always a church in context and in the period of modernity. The church is a secularized church. Secularization determines the identity of the church; the church is not a ghetto in modernity. The church is more secularized than it gives itself out to be and more 'modern' than it would like.

> In view of this situation it does not make much sense to join in the anti-Modernist lament which is again very popular in Catholic circles today, as if modern culture were simply from the devil and there were no longer any bridges, any points of contact in it, for the Christian message. By no means! This culture too is included in the saving work of Christ, and it too needs to have the gospel preached to it in an inviting sympathy; it too belongs to the universal community of all children of God on the way to the promised kingdom of God.[4]

This quotation from the Frankfurt dogmatic theologian Medard Kehl makes it clear that modern culture and Christian religion stand in a reciprocal relationship, and even more strongly that modernity also knows promises which bring us a little bit nearer to the 'kingdom of God'. In other words, whether one speaks of an emphasis on personal conscience or individual freedom, tolerance towards other basic convictions or plurality, scepticism towards an absolutist claim to validity or criticism as a standpoint in life, many values which modern society takes for granted correspond to the values of the Judaeo-Christian tradition. And this compatibility is not fortuitous, but causal. For just as modern culture is 'infected' by Christianity, so Christianity is infected by modern culture. Even secularized societies are not automatically irreligious, nor do they 'abstain' from the church. They produce secularized forms of religion and interpretations of the tradition, and in their departure from the tradition they open up a prospect for the traditions of Christianity.

This article is neither a lament for modernity nor a panegyric on it; rather, it is about the fascinating question of how the church itself is 'modern' and how it reacts to the problem of a secularized society. I am answering this question by a discussion of church ministries, because they represent the church in society. Ministries are public functions in and by which the church articulates its specific understanding of itself. They document the presence of the church in society, i.e. in a society which wants to limit religion to the private sphere. From a church perspective the question is the dramatic one whether the church is content with the status of 'private church' which has been assigned to it, or whether it goes on the offensive in finding itself a place in modern society.

Now we are accustomed to locating the question of ministry in the

Catholic Church primarily in the area of dogmatics. In the question of the ordination of women that has led to our submitting to a particular dogmatic theological pattern of argumentation. The consequence of this is that current discussion is primarily about whether it was Jesus' will for women to be ordained priests, whether the church has the authority to decide to give women an ordained ministry, and how one is to assess the fact that the biblical witnesses speak of twelve apostles but grant only one woman the title 'apostle of the apostles'. In other words, the investigation is into whether there are supports either for or against a ministerial priesthood of women in *the* tradition. Now as early as 1932, Edith Stein, who is above any suspicion of feminism, remarked on the question of the ordination of women: 'In dogmatic terms, nothing seems to me to stand in the way, nothing that could prevent the church from carrying out such an unprecedented innovation . . .'[5] This is a view which the great Catholic theologian Karl Rahner shared.[6] Moreover an almost unanimous opinion by the Papal Biblical Commission, when asked for their view about the biblical basis for assessing the priestly ordination of women, says 'that a prohibition of the ordination of women priests cannot be read out of holy Scripture'.[7] The papal letter *Ordinatio sacerdotalis* of 30 May 1994 puts us in a position in which the discussion of the ordination of women is forbidden. This document pursued the aim 'of shifting the debate from the level of practical reasons for or against the ordination of women priests . . . to the level of the formal problem. The intervention of the magisterial authority was such as to turn a substantive question into a question of obedience . . . a not untypical procedure in the crises of modernization in the church.'[8] So theological discussion is no longer on the question of a historical reconstruction of the church's ministry but also on the question of obedience towards the magisterium. Thus this question becomes a *status confessionis* (= a criterion by which orthodoxy is measured).

My comments are governed by an interest in reflecting on diversity of forms of ministry in their function as a public representation of the church. The content and justification for the forms of ministry are characterized by a concern for the church to be made visible in postmodern society. So the starting point for giving a basis for church ministries lies in the sociology of religion and not in a reconstruction of tradition and scripture. That does not mean that the arguments from tradition and scripture are bracketed off, but the questions asked are about the function of ministries in a secularized society. It is a matter of the church going on the offensive in the debate, the breaking down of polarizations and the abandonment of a purely defensive scheme of reaction.[9]

I shall do this in three stages. First I shall describe the transition from a modern to a postmodern society, i.e. the examination of individualization as a social form. In order to break up the customary identification of the church with tradition and society with modernity, I shall describe process of modernization in the church. As a second stage I shall introduce models of the church from the feminist theological debate orientated on persons and relationships, which attempt to respond to the social processes of modernization. The summary of this debate issues in a plea for different forms of ministry, or a reflection on the variety of the church's ministry. In a third stage I shall attempt to reflect on this multiplicity in the context of already existing ministries and new ministries which need to be created; this is expressed in the juxtaposition of diaconate, presbyterate and koinonate.

What is a modern society?

Descriptions of modern society are usually made in terms of society, culture and the individual. Thus the sociologist and theologian Karl Gabriel mentions three elements in a description of modernity. First, the 'gradual differentiation and rationalization of functional systemic structures in the sphere of rule, religion, economy and science'.[10] In other words, modern society has different sub-systems with their own codes, and laws which exist independently of one another. Secondly, the pluralization and criticism of traditions. In other words, unitary traditional patterns of interpretation are replaced by a multiplicity of cultural patterns of interpretation. And thirdly, the liberation of individuals from traditional bonds of origin, status and religion. Thus individuality becomes something like a socially ordained form of life in industrial society. More and more people are now required to do what was expected of and allowed to only a few, namely to live their own lives. In this way individualization in an industrial society is 'institutionalized' and is no longer the decision of the individual. That has various consequences, one of them being that there are no longer individual subjects, like the worker, the citizen, the Christian, the lay person, the husband, the wife. 'Patchwork identities' are developed which are described by the process of becoming a self in the various sub-systems of society and integrated by the individual. In other words, the individual is required to sense the dissolution of social forms not only as a collapse but also as a departure for new shores. It is clear that gain and loss are very close together here. The process of becoming replaces the process of being. In this logic of individualization one can remark, in a version of Simone de Beauvoir's famous saying 'One does not come into the world a woman, one becomes one',[11] that one does not come into the world a Christian but becomes one. It is a task and an opportunity for the individual to 'sketch out' and to realize his or her biography. Identity can no longer be safeguarded on the level of simple role identity. 'All role identities, even those distributed by the market, come under the pressure of reflection and must be reconstructed on a "self-referential" basis at a second level – the identity of the self.'[12] Gabriel calls this diagnosis of the individual in modern society the 'breakthrough to developed modernity'. But what is a developed modernity, as opposed to a less developed modernity?

From modern to postmodern society

I would like to dwell for a moment on the distinction between developed and less developed modernity or modern and postmodern society. In his book 'Risk Society. On the Way to Another Modernity', the sociologist Ulrich Beck descries society by distinguishing between reflective and simple modernity:

> The 'tradition' of industrial society has taken the place of premodernity. If at the beginning of the nineteenth century the forms of life and work in a feudal agricultural society were being replaced, today those of a developed industrial society are being replaced: social classes and strata, small families with the 'normal biographies' of men and women who have entered them . . . That is demystifying a legend which was invented in the nineteenth century and still dominates thought and action in science, politics and everyday life – namely the legend that in its scheme of work and life industrial society is a modern society.[13]

Beck points on the one hand to a historically familiar scheme which understands the feudal agricultural society as 'premodern' in contrast to 'modern' industrial society. On the other hand he points out that the industrial society which arrived to modernize the tradition has itself already become tradition again. In other words, he sees a process of modernization of industrial society at work which he calls 'reflective' modernity. His theory of society is based on the assessment 'that we are eyewitnesses – subject and object – of a break within modernity which is detaching itself from the contours of classical industrial society and shaping a new form – what is here called the (industrial) "risk society"'.'[14] With the term 'risk society' the author wants to indicate the dangers and crises of industrial society. In simple modernity one could still believe that technology served progress, that more investment created jobs, that interest in religion was declining. In reflective modernity one could become aware that technology also destroys the basis of life, destroy jobs, and not going to church is not to be identified with a lack of religion. These risks are publicly pilloried in the social movements (the women's movement, the peace movement and the environmental movement). Beck sees these 'anti-publics' or the promoters of a 'politics of counter-interpretation' not as slips in modernity but as a postmodern mouthpiece for a criticism of science, technology, progress and culture which formulates a consistent further development beyond the scheme of industrial society.'[15] For Beck, the (self-)criticism of industrial society represents a modernization of the tradition of industrial society. Here he uses the term 'reflective modernity' – the theologian Gabriel would say developed modernity – and not postmodernity because he sees the risk society as involved in modernity and going beyond modernity. It can also be said that modernity is coming into conflict with its own principles. Democracy so to speak always also provokes criticism of it. Accordingly the modernization of democratic industrial society means publicly criticizing the halving of its principles. Reflective or developed modernity consumes the fruits of modernity, and to this degree continuity and contradiction can be seen in the 'post-'. Now a developed postmodern society is not a homogenous form either. The development from a modern to a postmodern society does not follow the scheme of a temporal chronology but always also displays breaks, reversals and time-lags. One need only think of German reunification. Simply in terms of the German-speaking world it can be demonstrated that we live in a society which tends to be postmodern with partially premodern, partially modern and partially postmodern features.

Modernization in the Catholic Church

If we now look at the development of the Catholic Church and Christian theology in this century, here similarly we can note a contemporaneity of traditionality and modernity. That creates tensions and contradictions which in part are to be derived from factors dependent on the context of modern industrial society and the postmodern service-industry society. With reference to magisterial statements of the First and Second Vatican

Councils I shall now mention developments which document the entry of modernity into the church. As a second step I shall mention contradictions which are connected with unresolved questions 'at home'.

Two dogmatic constitutions were passed at the First Vatican Council which are remarkable from a present-day perspective, since their theme is potential conflict which still dogs the church today. These are the constitution *Dei Filius*, which discusses the relationship between modern science and Christian faith, and asserts that they are compatible, and the constitution *Pater Aeternus*, which defines the pope's primacy of jurisdiction and the infallibility of his magisterium.

> Anyone who goes through the content of the church's scheme and perceives its thrust will easily recognize the *Sitz im Leben* of the view of the church. It is directed primarily against state churches, which oppressed the free self-determination of the church, and against that liberalism which relativized the authority of the church and the need of it for salvation, in favour of an individualistic practice of religion left to private judgment and personal choice. The anti-Protestant accent which is also present was above all connected with the view that the root of liberalism lay in Protestantism and its denial of the authority and infallibility of the church.[16]

The modern world is explained in terms of denial of the authority of the hierarchical church. The church sees itself in competition with other confessions, the state, the sciences and other world-views. But the Council sees the root of all 'modern' evil in the appeal by the individual subject to his own reason and decision. From the perspective of the Council the 'primacy of reason', which dominated the sciences as rationalism, and the 'spirit of freedom and independence from any authority' which was expressed in liberalism, are the main points of criticism of modernity.[17] Let us recall the three characteristics of a modern society: the differentiation of social sub-systems, cultural pluralization and growing individualization. That makes it clear that Vatican I perceived these processes of modernization very clearly, though it evaluated them in a negative way.

> What is lamented in the particularization of the church is the consequence of the differentiation of social sub-systems, each of which claims autonomy for itself. In the philosophical and ideological systems which the Council condemns, there appears the cultural pluralization which goes along with critical and detached reflection

on the traditions that have been handed down. And when the Council sees at work here the pernicious arrogance of the individual who puts his private judgment above church authority, it is perceiving the process of growing individualization.[18]

Even if we have to concede that Vatican I primarily identifies the shadow side of modernity and utters polemic against it, it is extremely interesting to note that the criticism formulated here was taken up a century later by the new social movements and base church movements. The overvaluation of rationality, the pressure towards an objective explanation of the world by the sciences, the boundless belief in progress, the establishment of the modern 'male-bourgeois' subject as the subject which controlled nature, this is the material from which the opposition movements of this century formed. Even if the church of the nineteenth century 'by its attitude made a major contribution to the view that the emancipation of human beings could be established only in the face of the church and Christianity',[19] and thus helped to cause the confrontation between modernity and tradition, it cannot be overlooked that on the other hand the politics of modernity was governed by a fundamental hostility to religion and the church.

The programme of the Second Vatican Council (1962–1965) can be summed up under the headings 'dialogue with the world' and 'renewal of the church'. Furthermore, this council states 'that it is essential for the church to be in the world'.[20] The dogmatic constitution *Lumen Gentium* ('On the church') is set alongside the pastoral constitution *Gaudium et spes* ('The church in today's world'). The social-historical aspect and the transcendental dimension of the church are defined as being interlocked and not strictly separate – as was still the case at the First Vatican Council. The development of modernity is no longer seen as a history of decline but as a challenge with opportunities and risks. Whereas Vatican I still saw the coming into being of human subjects who express themselves in a claim to freedom as the root of all the evil of modernity, Vatican II saw this in a positive light: it accords with human dignity and the will of God. The church is understood as the church in modernity. It is no longer regarded as the superior mistress of humankind, but as the community of the people of God. Vatican II wanted to get away from a legalistic and clerical conception to a communitarian conception.

From a present-day perspective it remains to ask whether the Council succeeded here. One may be convinced that the constitution on the church, *Lumen gentium*, legitimates both ecclesiologies. That this double structure is split is shown by the conflicts after the Council. 'Is the church a pyramidal-hierarchical entity, or is the notion of *communio fidelium* a more adequate description of the church? *Lumen gentium* sketches out both ecclesiologies.'[21] Thus for the post-conciliar movements (the lay movement, the peace movement, the women's movement and the 'we are the church' movement), the Catholic Church

> has still not sufficiently decisively given up its premodern form, whereas for the traditionalists the future of the church lies only in a return to its pre-conciliar form. It is obvious to the church leaders that the main cause of the crisis is to be seen in the social environment of unbelief and the uncontrolled growth of theological ideas or bold new practices . . . For charismatic movements, prayer groups and meditation circles, by contrast, the present-day crisis of the church primarily lies in a coldness of faith, a lack of devotion, spirituality and religious experience. However, for politically committed Christians it is evident that the main cause of the present-day crisis in the church lies in the uncritical adoption of the modern division of work (religion for the private sphere, for the church sphere, for the feelings) and in the *laissez-faire* juxtaposition of church and state, church and society, church and politics.[22]

So one can be convinced that relationship between the church and modernity as stated in ecclesiology is ambiguous and see the controversy over the right understanding of the church as a more recent Modernist crisis.[23]

But one can also be convinced that the reality of the church in a postmodern form can be read off the existence side by side of different models (*societas perfecta*, mystical body of Christ, fellowship of believers, women's church).

On the way to a postmodern church?

If we consider all the current eschatological diagnoses of the church, the suspicion arises that here we no longer have a more or less unconscious continuation of the secularization thesis of the 1980s; rather, this diagnosis relates to a less developed modernity. In other words, if modernity itself has become a problem, is regarded as a 'risk society' (Beck), or if attention is drawn to the qualitative difference between reflective and simple modernity (Gabriel), we may expect that such a recognition will also find its way into the analysis of the church.

Theologians tend to see the future of the church in the 'end of the clerical church'. Others prescribe radical reform cures for the 'church in a coma'.[24] The church situation is described as perplexing and hopeless:

> One of the central problems of the Catholic Church in Germany today may suffice as an example of the perplexing contemporary situation, namely the overinstitutionalization of the church. Here traditional Catholic church theology, a renewed understanding of the church and several lines of modernization are fused into a new explosive form of being the church. On the one hand the notions of the hierarchical character of the church and of the church as an autonomous saving institution ordained by God continue. On the other hand, especially in the context of a renewed understanding of the church, particular factors of modernity are having an influence in an unexpected way (the differentiation and segmenting of society, and hence the detachment of faith from the church, bureaucratization as an expression of modern purposive rationality, the centralization of church organization, individualization, and a removal of faith from the cult into ethics and education). All this taken together results in a new form of being the church which will only increase the perplexity of church members because of the intrinsic ambivalence.[25]

This condition is 'confusing' if one remains imprisoned in a 'modern diagnosis' of the church and society which goes by polarization. From a postmodern perspective one can note how these different forms of being the church exist side by side and are interwoven. The contradictory character of the church no longer results in an 'either-or' but in a 'both-and'.

Women's church and women in the church

Depending on the way in which they interpret their situation in life and the perspective they develop, people favour particular models of the church. Those who are involved in questions of developmental policy or the protection of the environment share a bond which transcends the classic confessional boundaries more than any dogmatic doctrines. Constantly new 'confessions' are forming across the old confessions along with the interpretation of the situation of the church and theology.[26]

This means that social changes and contradictions themselves become factors in the formation of new confessions. That is certainly true of the women's liberation movement. Feminism arose out of the contradictions of modernity which apply to women in a special way. The promise of freedom, equality and solidarity seem to stop at the female sex. The entry of women into universities and the professional world and their right to vote did not bring the women of this century the equal opportunities that they hoped for of a self-determined life in church and society. The increasing activity of women in the professions did not mean that they were freed from the burdens of housekeeping and bringing up children. Talk of the 'double burden' is an indication of this. Women had the experience that reconciling professional work and bringing up children was regarded as a woman's problem and not as the expression of a society which was not ready to see bringing up children and housework as work. Questions were asked about the social distribution of power, and this led to feminists no longer 'asking' just for participation in social tasks but wanting to change society in such a way that the work of relationship and profession was borne by all. The churches and theology, too, did not escape this uproar.

The displacement of church and religion from almost all spheres of public life in the process of secularization has led to women becoming the ones who hand on religious awareness and engage in religious upbringing. A 'feminizing of religion' has been noted at the end of the nineteenth century and the beginning of the twentieth. This is assessed in various ways. Thus the historian Irmtraud Götz von Olenhusen sees a 'retraditionalizing of the female role'[27] at work in the close connection between women and religion and a process of liberation from traditions which have been handed down in the withdrawal of men from religious involvement. By contrast, her colleague Barbara Welter sees the feminizing of religion as a tendency to radicalize women, as it were an 'involuntary modernization'.[28] Götz von Olenhusen uses a standard argument to stamp church and religion as an oppressive tradition: 'The Catholic Church still maintains the church as a male alliance; women are still excluded from the ordained ministry.'[29] Today we face a situation in which the close relationship between women and religion has remained in a numerical comparison with men, as is reflected in the talk of the women's church in the men's church,[30] but the tendency of women between eighteen and fifty to leave the church is increasing. 'We are the church of women not in exile but in exodus,'[31] is the way in which Rosemary Radford Ruether describes the situation. Ten years ago Christian women found their situation in the church captured in the image of the exodus community. The exodus community illustrates the contemporaneity of movements of exodus and new beginnings. Other images followed like 'sisterhood as a cosmic alliance',[32] as a 'community of friends',[33] as 'confederates',[34] 'communities of resistance and solidarity',[35] 'the church in the round'[36] and 'discipleship of equals'.[37] If we read these images against the background of descriptions of the processes of modernization, it is striking how they reflect a democratic and egalitarian structural aspect and individualization as a social form. All these images are discussed under the heading 'ekklesia of women', which is understood as 'critical praxis and vision of a radical democracy in society and religion'.[38] Accordingly ekklesia designates the 'democratic-public alliance of free citizens who insist that women must become visible in the sphere of biblical religion'.[39] One could even say that the ekklesia of women is a postmodern concept of the church. It takes for granted the achievements of modernity: it is grounded in an egalitarian view of structures, a multiplicity of ecclesiological images and a concern to make the church visible in different formations of ministry.

Elements of a feminist theology of the ministry

In the current feminist theological debate there is little sign of making the ordination of women a central theme in the discussion. One can assess this, as Ida Ramin does, as a reflex action to the ban on discussion ordained by the pope, as a kind of self-deformation of the excluded,[40] or alternatively as a refusal to fight for a ministry in which there is little place for the realities of women's life. What some regard as a refusal to fight for the ordination of women is regarded by others from the perspective of the danger of an integration of women into ministries stamped with patriarchy. 'Therefore while the ordination of women can serve as a means of changing patriarchal-clerical structures, at the same time it can contribute towards consolidating these structures.'[41] This standpoint points to the contradictory situation of present-day feminism, which represents both a radical concept and a commonplace truth. 'Feminism is the radical notion that women are people.'[42] Reference to the great diversity in the church's ministry could resolve this dilemma.[43] This diversity can be justified both from the perspective of Christian tradition and also from the requirements of the church in a modern society. If the whole discussion on the priestly ministry for women concentrates on the demand to participate in the existing ministry, both sides remain stuck in a 'premodern' figure of argumentation.

So the question of the ordained ministry for women is not just a fundamental ecclesiological question, it is not just a 'women's problem', but an inquiry into the theological self-understanding of the church in postmodernity. The battle against the ordination of women can also be seen as a 'rearguard action'. Just as it is insufficient to champion the 'femininity of God' in the face of the domination of 'male' images of God,[44] so it is insufficient to call for an admission of women to the priestly ministry which does not reflect the 'fundamental nature of the church's ministry' or distorts the perspective on the multiplicity of forms of ministry. The answer to the question of the church's self-understanding depends on the image of the church emphasized at the time, which may be governed e.g. by the reconstruction of early Christian history, or the line of argument taken by magisterial documents, ecumenical dialogue or liturgical practice.[45] The consensus of all these analyses is an emphasis on the character of church ministries as service and the wish for them all to express the universal priesthood of all believers. Two paradigms can be discerned in the feminist theological discussion, which relate to this consensus: (a) the paradigm of service and partnership, and (b) the paradigm of shared or contextual pastoral care.

Letty Russell points out that the vocation to the ministry is not an option for some Christian women, but is an essential element in the Christian existence which tries to take the form of partnerships in the ministry of Christ.[46] Other women theologians recall Jesus' washing of the disciples' feet at the Last Supper, an action in which the character of the church's ministry as service is expressed much more strongly than in presiding at the eucharist.[47] All these authors reject a hierarchical sacerdotal view in favour of a functional communitarian model. The content of this last model is supplied with the term diakonia, which is either located in the theology of discipleship of Jesus or developed biblically (Luke 4.18–19). Here diakonia symbolizes a vision of mutality and solidarity,[48] partnership and service. It is understood as a dimension of the ministry and not presented as a separate form of ministry.

The paradigm of shared pastoral care is really an 'argument' from a pastoral praxis which is already being experienced. In other words, it has long been experienced that the church's ministry has fanned out, and the notion of the church's ministry as a 'total role in one hand' is seen as an outdated development. The main image of the church in feminist theological discussion is a 'discipleship of equals'. This image excludes a first- and a second-class ministry.[49]

The diverse forms of church ministry

Now the question remains what forms of ministry reflect the 'discipleship of equals' which the Second Vatican Council reflects on in *Lumen gentium* as the 'universal priesthood' of all believers. 'By divine institution holy Church is ordered and governed with a wonderful diversity . . . In Christ and in the Church there is, then, no inequality arising from race or nationality, social condition or sex.'[50]

Karl Rahner begins from the fundamental character of the church as ministry, which he wants to make public and visible. 'Wherever a special function in the church is necessary in an intensive, significant and permanent way, we have something like a ministry.'[51] Rahner's understanding of ministry begins from the image of the church as the people of God. For him it is clear that 'the holy community of believers as an irreversible victorious presence of God's statement of himself is ontologically and logically prior to ministry in the church . . . That already follows from the fact that according to Catholic principles office can be held only by those who are baptized, and therefore belong to the community of believers.' Ministry in the church is primarily guided 'by the sociological necessities and needs of the church as the totality of concrete communities'.[52] For Rahner the community is not an organization of individual Christians but a sacramental community of faith; as such it has a mission which must become visible. This making visible of the ministry is important both for the mission of Christ and for the needs of a concrete context of community and church. For Rahner these are not irreconcilable opposites. So in this sense the church has the fundamental character of ministry, which is made concrete when persons take part in this fundamental character of ministry, in other words are empowered for ministry.

If all pastoral ministries take part in the ministerial commission of the church, the question then is how this participation can be made visible. And if the 'sociological necessities of the church as the totality of the concrete community' are to be important, this can only result in a plea for diversity in forms of ministry.

The Bamberg pastoral theologian Ottmar Fuchs proposes a twofold ordained ministry: presbyterate and diaconate. Both have responsibility for (eucharistic) leadership and both are ordained states on an equal footing. He wants to see the church's ministry in that basic dual structure in which the presbyteral ministry takes on the dimension of martyria and the diaconal ministry the dimension of diakonia in the church. 'The equal status of the two spheres of ministry reflects the twofold commandment or nature of the church to love God and neighbour, martyria and diakonia.'[53] Here the diaconate is seen as 'an effective solidarity of the structural power of ministry with the poor and disadvantaged'; the presbyteral ministry is made 'responsible for representing Christ in word and sign'.[54] Thus the diaconal ministry can be understood as the 'representation of Christ' in the world, as a ministerial enabling of the church to make Christ visible in the diverse social sectors. So Fuchs is not arguing, as many dogmatic theologians do, for an integration of the diaconate into the *ordo* but for two ministries of equal status on the basis of a fundamentally dual structure of the one church ministry. He certainly succeeds in theologically revaluing the office of deacon, but he maintains a strict division between presbyteral and diaconal ministry.

The church as *communio*

It is striking that all the positions which argue for a diversity of forms of ministry do so on the basis of a leading idea of the Second Vatican Council, the 'communio church'. 'The *communio* ecclesiology is the central and fundamental idea of the council documents.'[55] *Communio* (*koinonia*) sums up the communal, brotherly and sisterly nature of a free collegial assembly. The Council elucidated the *communio* ecclesiology not only with the image of the body of Christ but also with that of the people of God.

> What is clear to us for the people of Israel and the Old Testament is also to be emphasized over against the view of salvation in Western theology with its markedly individualistic colouring. Only as members of the people of God do we share in redemption and live in accordance with our calling . . . In the constitution on the church the Council explicitly combines the idea of *communio* with the image of the 'people of God': 'Established by Christ as a communion of life, love and truth, it is taken up by him also as the instrument for the salvation of all; as the light of the world and the salt of the earth (cf. Matt. 5.13–16) it is sent forth in to the whole world' (LG 9).[56]

The term *communio* in *Lumen gentium* reflects the intention of first emphasizing in the church that common element for which all are called and are sent, and only then speaking of specific tasks and functions. The problem now is that in the church documents not only do several images of the church stand side by side (body of Christ, people of God); they are set over against each other in the praxis of the church. As soon as the concrete question is 'the definition of the ecclesiological place of the ordained ministry and the non-ordained ministries, the hierarchical legalistic model for the church proves not yet to have been written off'.[57] So there is a differentiated subordination of specific tasks within the common sending of all believers. The *communio* ecclesiology is by no means just the concept of a 'church from below' as a community with a democratic structure, but it is not the concept of a 'church from above' as a community conceived of in hierarchical terms either. This is a picture of the church as 'church from within',[58] and so the question is 'what ecclesiological conclusions follow from the fact that the *communio* church has to bear witness to God's *communio*, its communal "power of attraction" and its communal "concern for involvement"'.[59] The character of the church as sacrament or its basic character as ministry owes itself precisely to the divine power of relationship which is manifested in the *communio*, i.e. is publicly visible. So if the church has to bear witness to God as *communio* then the testimony of the people of God may not be absent. In that case 'the universal priesthood of all believers' must also find its expression in the fact that being active in the church full time, part-time or in an honorary capacity has an ecclesiological relevance. In that case the commitment and competence of Christians in a postmodern society must also be given ministerial enabling, a public making visible of the church in different places.

Koinonate as ministerial enabling

A (post)modern society is characterized by being divided into different sub-areas. For the church that means the necessity of being present in these sub-areas. Theologians are working full time today in a variety of institutions: the social services, schools, hospitals, prisons, the media and universities. That means that the church is present in all these sub-areas without being 'visible'. The theologians work in these sectors under the conditions of these systems. Christian faith is handed down in our society more than ever by persons and less and less by institutions (like community, association, family). Individualization as a form of social life leads to Christians forming as a group under different perspectives from confessional perspectives. Alongside the identities determined by confession there are topics which arise out of social conflicts, like peace, women, the environment, anti-racism and a just world order, which become new factors in 'forming churches'. That means that the church happens in many places, and its contour is determined by a diversity of models. So it will be necessary not just to leave the 'representation of Christ' to a ministry or the personal efforts of individuals, but to give expression to the fundamental character of the church as ministry in different formations of ministry. The testimony of the 'communal concern for the will of God' needs to be given in different forms. What is needed is a ministerial enabling for the different areas of society.

Ministries in an institution like the church mean not only that everyone acts in a churchly way but that everyone acts responsibly as the church. The notion of *communio* was not only essential for the Second Vatican Council but also represents a tremendously important potential in a society which has said farewell to communal social forms and at the same time has a longing for them. What is there against Christians active in the different sub-spheres of society with commitment and competence joining together in a koinonate? What about transferring ministerial functions to individual Christians who are empowered here by the church? A koinonate would be a ministry which represents the church in the various sub-areas of society, and not just in the parishes. The various social fields of church involvement like work in the social sphere, culture, the media, prisons, hospitals and academic institutions could be perceived as places of pastoral care. The koinonate could be an attempt to go on the offensive in keeping the church present in many places. And it could get us out of the dead end of hierarchical and dual appointments to offices. The loss of function and relevance of the church and religion in a postmodern society can be countered by setting up public markers. In respect of the diaconate or a koinonate, that amounts to what the President of the Catholic Women's Alliance in Germany, Hanna-Renate Laurien, said at an international congress on the topic of 'Ministries in the Church': 'Whoever refuses to take the first step for fear of the tenth has no trust in God!'[60]

Translated by John Bowden

Notes

1. This is an abbreviated version of my article published in *Frauen zwischen Dienst und Amt. Frauenmacht und Ohnmacht in der Kirche*, Düsseldorf 1998, 85–113.

2. Thus the title of a book by the sociologist of religion Joachim Matthes, *Die Emigration der Kirche aus der Gesellschaft*, Hamburg 1964.

3. Johannes A. van der Ven, *Ecclesiologie in context. Handboek pratktische theologie*, Kampen 1993, 136.

4. Medard Kehl, *Wohin geht die Kirche? Eine Zeitdiagnose*, Freiburg im Breisgau 1996, 33.

5. Edith Stein, *Frauenbildung und Frauenberufe*, Munich [4]1956, 169.

6. Karl Rahner, 'Priestertum der Frau?', *Stimmen der Zeit* 102, 1977, 291–301.

7. A. Ebneter, 'Keine Frauen im Priesteramt', *Orientierung* 41, 1977, 25.

8. W. Gross (ed.), *Frauenordination. Stand der Diskussion in der Katholischen Kirche*, Munich 1996, 7–8.

9. Hermann-Josef Grosse Kracht, *Kirche in ziviler Gesellschaft. Studien zur Konfliktgeschichte von katholischer Kirche und demokratischer Öffentlichkeit*, Paderborn, Vienna, Munich and Zurich 1997, sheds light on the difference between the two strategies.

10. Karl Gabriel, *Christentum zwischen Tradition und Postmoderne*, Quaestiones Disputatae 141, Freiburg, Basel and Vienna 5/1996, 15.

11. Simone de Beauvoir, *The Second Sex*, London 1968.

12. Gabriel, *Christentum zwischen Tradition und Postmoderne* (n. 10), 141.

13. Ulrich Beck, *Risikogesellschaft. Auf dem Weg in eine andere Moderne*, Frankfurt 1986, 251.

14. Ibid., 13.

15. Ibid., 69.

16. Hermann J. Pottmeyer, 'Modernisierung in der katholischen Kirche', in Franz-Xaver Kaufmann and Arnold Zingerle (eds), *Vatikanum II und Modernisierung. Historische, theologische und sociologische Perspektiven*, Paderborn, Munich, Vienna and Zurich 1996, 131–46: 133.

17. Cf. Hermann J. Pottmeyer, *Der Glaube vor dem Anspruch der Wissenschaft. Die Konstitution über den katholischen Glauben Dei Filius des I. Vatikanischen Konzils und die unveröffentlichten theologischen Voten der vorbereitenden Kommission*, Freiburg 1968, 29–36.

18. Pottmeyer, 'Modernisierung in der katholischen Kirche' (n. 16), 133–4.

19. Ibid., 134.

20. Ibid., 139.

21. Hans-Georg Ziebertz, 'Kirchenprofile angehender Seelsorger', in id. (ed.), *Christliche Gemeinschaft vor einem neuen Jahrtausend. Strukturen-Subjekte-Kontexte*, Weinheim 1997, 11–34: 19.

22. Siegfried Wiedenhofer, 'Grundprobleme des katholischen Kirchenverständnisses im Übergang zu einer neuen epochalen Gestalt des Glaubens', in Carl Amery, Johann Baptist Metz et al., *Sind die Kirchen am Ende?*, Regensburg 1995, 129–57: 131.

23. Peter Hünermann, 'Droht eine dritte Modernisierungskrise? Ein offener Brief an den Vorsitzenden der Deutschen Bishofskonferenz, Karl Lehmann', *Herder-Korrespondenz* 43, 1989, 130–5.

24. Leo Karrer, *Aufbruch der Christen. Das Ende der klerikalen Kirche*, Munich 1989; Franz Köster, *Kirche im Koma*, Frankfurt am Main 1989.

25. Wiedenhofer, 'Grundprobleme des katholischen Kirchenverständnisses' (n. 22), 133–4.

26. Klaus Tanner, 'Protestantische Individualität und Kirche', in Amery and Metz, *Sind die Kirchen am Ende?* (n. 22), 110–28: 117.

27. Irmtraud Götz von Olenhusen, 'Die Feminisierung von Religion und Kirche im 19. und 20. Jahrhundert. Forschungsstand und Forschungsperspektiven', in *Frauen unter dem Patriarchat der Kirchen. Katholikinnen und Protestantinnen im 19. und 20. Jahrhundert*, Stuttgart, Berlin and Cologne 1995, 9–12.

28. Barbara Welter, ' "Frauenwille ist Gotteswille". Die Feminisierung der Religion in America', in Claudia Honegger and Barbara Heintz (eds), *Listen der Ohnmacht*, Frankfurt am Main 1981, 326–35: 316.

29. Götz von Olenhusen, 'Die Feminisierung von Religion und Kirche im 19. und 20. Jahrhundert' (n. 27), 16.

30. Bernadette Brooten and Norbert Greinacher, *Frauen in einer Männerkirche*, Munich 1982.

31. Rosemary Radford Ruether, *Unsere Wunden heilen, unsere Befreiung feiern. Rituale in der Frauenkirche*, Stuttgart 1988, 89.

32. Mary Daly, *Beyond God the Father*, Boston 1977.

33. Mary E. Hunt, *Fierce Tenderness: A Feminist Theology of Friendship*, New York 1991, 42.

34. The Dutch 'Women and Faith' movement uses this image: 'Confederates' are women in relationships of equal status who are also aware of their differences.

35. Sharon D. Welch, *A Feminist Ethic of Risk*, Minneapolis 1989.

36. Letty M. Russell, *Church in the Round: Feminist Interpretation of the Church*, Louisville 1993.

37. Elisabeth Schüssler Fiorenza, *In Memory of Her*, New York and London [2]1995, 97–235.

38. Ead., *Jesus, Miriam's Child, Sophia's Prophet: Critical Issues in Feminist Christology*, London 1995, 24.

39. Ead., *Bread Not Stone: The Challenge of Feminist Biblical Interpretation*, Edinburgh 1990.

40. Ida Raming, *Frauenbewegung und Kirche. Bilanz eines 25-jährigen Kampfes für Gleichberechtigung und Befreiung der Frau seit dem 2. Vatikanischen Konzil*, Weinhem 1989, 95.

41. Elisabeth Schüssler Fiorenza, 'Neutestamentlich-frühchristliche Argumente zum Thema Frau und Amt', *Theologische Quartalschrift* 173, 1993, 173–85: 173.

42. 'This popular tongue-in-cheek definition accentuates the irony that feminism in the twentieth century is both a radical concept and at the same time a "commonsense" notion', Elisabeth Schüssler Fiorenza, *Sharing Her Word. Feminist Biblical Interpretation in Context*, Boston 1998, 3–4.

43. Anne Marie Korte, 'De rode vlag op de ijsberg. De kwestie van "vrouwen in het ambt" kan worden verder gebracht door juist aandacht aan de verschillen te besteden', *de Bazuin*, 11 December 1992, 6–8.

44. Cf. My remarks on anti-modernism in feminist theology in *Zwischen lila und lavendel. Schritte feministischer Theologie*, Regensburg 1996, 85–6.

45. The different lies of argumentation can be found in Gross, *Frauenordination* (n. 8).

46. Russell, *Church in the Round* (n. 36), 50.

47. Lynn N. Rhodes, *Co-Creating. A Feminist Vision of Ministry*, Philadelphia 1987, 50.

48. Ibid., 133.

49. Elisabeth Schüssler Fiorenza, *Discipleship of Equals. A Critical Feminist Ekklesia-logy of Liberation*, New York and London 1993, 300.

50. *Lumen gentium* 32.

51. Paul M. Zulehner, *Denn du kommst unserem Tun mit deiner Gnade zuvor. Zur Theologie der Seelsorge heute. Paul M. Zulehner im Gespräch mit Karl Rahner*, Düsseldorf 1984, 89.

52. Ibid., 82.

53. Fuchs 1963, 67.

54. Ibid., 72.

55. Walter Kasper (ed.), *Zukunft aus der Kraft des Konzils. Die ausserordentliche Bischofssynode '85*, Freiburg 1986, 33.

56. Hermann J. Pottmeyer, 'Kirche als communio', *Bibel und Liturgie* 63, 1980, 2–9: 6.

57. Bernd Jochen Hilberath, 'Zum ekklesiologischen Ort der "Laien im pastoralen Dienst". Vorbemerkung zum kirchlichen und gesellschaftlichen Ort dogmatische Theologie', in Bernhard von Fraling et al (eds), *Kirche und Theologie im gesellschaftlichen Dialog*, Freiburg im Breisgau 1994, 370.

58. Ibid., 371.

59. Jürgen Werbick, *Kirche. Ein ekklesiologischer Entwurf für Studium und Praxis*, Freiburg, Basel and Vienna 1994, 346.

60. Quoted from *Rheinische Post*, 5 April 1997, 24.

Tracking the Ways of Women in Religious Leadership

Melanie A. May

'Read . . . like a tracker: with your eyes on the ground and the horizon simultaneously'

(Hannah Nyala[1])

A war over 'women's place' is being waged world-wide. Whether in Japan or India, Afghanistan or Israel, Uzbekhistan or the United States, debates about women's sexuality, reproductive power, and social and economic roles are not only heated but often violent.[2] These debates are integrally and intimately informed by religion. Indeed, the recently resurgent fundamentalist movements in Christianity, Islam, Judaism and Hinduism adamantly insist that religion *not* be separated from social structures and values as they have been in 'godless' modern Western societies.[3] These movements are committed to the restoration of women to our 'proper place' at home to care for children, while protected and provided for by our husbands. Within this world-view, women's leadership in religious communities is not only severely limited: the presence of women in leadership roles is a key indicator of the perceived 'godlessness' of more liberal religious communities.

Ironically, when the actual practice of women in religious leadership is investigated, 'liberal' and 'conservative' or fundamentalist religious communities are more similar than their formal rules and rhetoric suggest. Although most 'liberal' Christian and Jewish denominations in the United States have passed policies to enable women to carry out ordained ministries, studies conducted over the last twenty years unfailingly clarify the considerable obstacles yet to be overcome, e.g., placement difficulties, 'stained-glass ceilings', salary inequities, resistance to new styles of ministry and leadership.[4] Indeed, one recent study argues that denominations' decisions about women's religious leadership are symbolic gestures intended more to construct a public identity relative to wider cultural currents than to support women's full gender equality with men in leadership roles.[5] Another recent study argues that even this formal structural support for women's leadership is being eroded as 'liberal' denominations are restructuring ministry in ways that marginalize women, e.g., more part-time positions, more partially or non-stipendiary positions, more ordination tracks to institute a new hierarchy of specialized ministries,[6] more retired male ministers and priests used as an alternative labour supply.[7]

The intensity of today's debates, together with the intricacy of backlash dynamics, make it clear that what is at stake is not only 'women's place' in various religious communities. What is at stake is the very future of religious communities – their religious imagery, practices, discourses – together with the future of the surrounding social structures and sanctions governing men's and women's places. In short, the backlash is a barometer indicating that the pressure brought to bear on religious and social structures of male power and privilege is shaking the foundations.

This perspective on what is at stake makes it possible, indeed imperative, to speak about practices for transformation. This is to say, while clear-sightedness in the midst of backlash is crucial, we women risk our power to resist 'what is' if we do not also dare to articulate and act on what we hope will be, i.e., if we do not also practise, and proclaim, transformation. We do indeed need to keep our 'eyes on the ground and the horizon simultaneously'. On the horizon, the transformation to which we are called has at its heart radical redistribution – of power and privilege, and of roles and resources. Here, acknowledging, but not bound by, the backlash, I attempt to track ways in which I see women in religious leadership living – however haltingly, for living 'as if' is always ambivalent – into such a radically new reality, religiously and socially.

I do so convinced that the current ethos of exclusion[8] – exclusion of those who challenge what passes as the reigning religious and social consensus – is itself evidence that there is no going back. Exclusion, like other forms of outright and unreasoning repression, is born of desperation. For exclusion most often follows an era of radical inclusion, just as it is most often attended by talk about scarcity, attested by a widening abyss between those who are stock-piling and those who are falling through cracks.

The current ethos of exclusion is another indicator to me that a twenty-first-century view of the twentieth century in the United States will remark on a shift in the life of religious communities during the decade of the 1970s. During that decade, women emerged into religious leadership with unprecedented visibility and voice. Unprecedented numbers of women were ordained as pastors, and became professors in seminaries and divinity schools. Moreover, women began to be prominently represented among the officers of ecclesial and ecumenical organizations and institutions. This was not, of course, the circumstance for all women. Still today, in some churches and other religious communities, women are not ordained or authorized as leaders. Nonetheless, I believe a twenty-first-century view of this century will verify the tide-turning significance of the 1970s as an era of unprecedented inclusivity in the religious history of the United States, especially with regard to women's leadership in Jewish and in Christian communities.

But women clergy today are moving beyond inclusivity, 'are creating a new situation in many ways',[9] in the words of Zikmund, Lummis and Chang. In this new situation, women face a critical choice anew: will we accept and try to negotiate our way amid male-crafted, and usually male-dominated, paradigms and practices of religious leadership? Will we choose to create new forms of leadership, living as if and already into a new reality marked by radical redistribution of power and privilege, roles and resources? To track ways in which I see women practising transformation is to choose to create anew.

I. Research of the past, research for the future

One way in which women are living into radical newness is signalled by the leadership of women scholars. Women's retrieval of our religious leadership through the centuries of Jewish and Christian history certifies our contemporary practice by creating a tradition for it. Since refutations of women's ordination by the Roman Catholic and Orthodox Churches, among others, have most often appealed to an alleged two thousand years of unbroken tradition in which men only have been ordained, such scholarship is indeed foundation-shaking. This is to say, women's religious leadership that emerged with striking significance in the 1970s was not altogether unprecedented. Its significance was a numerical significance that spilled into new inclusivity. Since the 1970s, twenty years of scholarship has made clear that women in the earliest centuries of the Christian movement were martyrs and virgins, widows and deacons, prophets and householders.[10] Some scholars argue that these roles were in many instances consecrated, perhaps ordained, ecclesiastical offices.[11]

Twenty years of scholarship has also clarified that there was a prophetic succession in which women were prominent leaders alongside the apostolic succession that is often a reason for the refusal to ordain women. And this scholarship has explored more fully and clearly the women who were pioneer religious leaders in nineteenth-century America, women who opened the way for women in the 1970s.[12]

A review of this research into the past confirms that women's religious leadership through the centuries was sanctioned more often by a direct experience of the divine than by virtue of office or order. 'In the study of world religions,' writes Catherine Wessinger, 'a search for women as religious leaders inevitably leads to charismatic women who are saints, shamans, healers . . . recent scholarship has amply demonstrated that in mainstream religious traditions most women are marginalized.'[13]

Since the 1970s, however, more and more women have become religious leaders whose authority is legitimated officially and publicly. Indeed, the gains have been so significant that a key question driving recent research for the future is whether women in official positions of religious leadership are making a difference. If so, what difference does it make that women in significant numbers are prominently represented among religious leaders? Do women have different styles of leadership, styles sometimes said to be more egalitarian, personable, relational, and intuitive than men? Do women preach differently? Offer pastoral care differently? Have different views of spirituality? Responses to these and related questions are varied at this point.[14] For good reason, I think. In so far as women now face a critical choice as to whether we will accept *status quo* paradigms and practices or create new forms of religious leadership, the only responsible reading at this juncture is an ambivalent reading. To speak about signs of transformation is to speak in hope, is to live 'as if', convinced that this proclamation is itself creative of the radical new reality longed for.

II. 'As if' ambivalence

Interestingly, sociologists are taking the lead in exploring the question about the difference women are making. For example, Frederick W. Schmidt in his recent study of Protestant clergywomen identifies various ways in which women are choosing to relate to religious roles and institutions. Some women clergy function as effective leaders while still considering themselves to be 'outsiders' in their religious communities. Other women leaders are less alienated, but are nonetheless 'disengaged' from certain structures which, they feel, constrain them. Many women feel 'threatened' in relation to institutions in which most women still never move beyond entry-level positions. A handful of women clergy choose the role of 'reformer' and commit themselves to change. Many more choose to become 'conformist' in the hope that they will thereby survive as leaders within institutional and official structures.[15]

The stories being told by women are less ambiguous than the results of sociological studies.[16] These stories feature the price women are paying more than the difference women are making. Women speak of struggle more than of change. Specifically, as noted above, women continue to encounter resistance to their religious leadership. Women continue to be underpaid and overused. Women are insufficiently supported by structures still pervaded by practices that privilege men. Women are disproportionately placed in the poorest and smallest and most remote parishes. Women put up with long delays in attaining new placements and often hit 'the stained-glass ceiling' by the second move, or remain on the 'sticky floors' of entry-level wages and lateral moves. Women continue to deal with sexual harassment and abuse by male colleagues. For example, a survey released last spring revealed at 40% of women priests in the Church of England had experienced verbal abuse and 23% sexual harassment. Some women priests reported being spat at in the street.[17]

Not surprisingly, more and more Protestant clergy women are leaving parish ministry, even as the number of women students in theological schools continues to rise.[18] The women who leave parish ministry often get specialized training to work as ministers in other settings, e.g., in hospitals, hospices, nursing homes, college campuses, or the military as chaplains. They also often work as pastoral counsellors. In each instance, it is interesting to note, care-giving is valued more highly than the hierarchical power to control that often typifies leadership expectations in traditional religious institutions.

If I am talking like this, why do I still attempt to track ways in which women are practising transformation? I persist because it is precisely in the midst of the problems that women are often being most creative in producing new forms of religious leadership and religious community. For example, some women intentionally choose to create alternative models of ministry by stitching together several sorts of responsibility, combining part-time paid or voluntary work in a religious setting with a secular job. African-American women are especially and enormously creative, too often of necessity. Excluded from placement in many historic Black churches, African-American women mentor one another, formally and informally, and distinguish themselves time and again in founding churches and forms of ministry that move across traditional demarcations of religious and social. Although many women admit that such arrangements stretch the limits of their time and energy, one woman rabbi also remarked: '. . . cobbling together part-time positions delights me . . . it allows a cross fertilization that is extraordinarily fruitful'.[19] In short, women's choice to engage the 'as if' ambivalence that characterizes the present is often also a choice to resist traditional identities and roles. And such resistance may clear a way through the underbrush of backlash to open the possibility for participation in new creation.

III. The practice of presence

Amid this minefield of possibilities and problems, the practice of presence is one of the most powerful ways women are living into a new reality. One way in which I see women practising presence is as women are creating spaces in which we can be visible and voiced to one another and as new corporate bodies. Women in the 1990s are forming new coalitions and new communities dedicated to trespassing lines and walls set up by ecclesial and societal structures to keep the disadvantaged, often especially women, apart and therefore absent from one another. Many, although not all, of these coalitions and communities bring women together across dividing lines of race, ethnicity, class and sexual orientation. These new coalitions and new communities support and sustain our resistance, so our resistance can also become our choice to create rather than to pay the price of integration into dominant institutions and orders.

This is not, of course, a new strategy. During the nineteenth century in the United States, women's voluntary associations proliferated and were dedicated to moral and social reform, to overseas and domestic mission, to women's suffrage, etc.[20] In the twentieth century, most especially during the decade of the 1970s, women again created separate spaces for women. Although these spaces were separate, their primary purpose was usually not to be separatist, but to nurture women in ways not available or adequate in 'mainstream' religious communities and institutions. Indeed, women's presence in women's spaces often made it possible for women to continue to be present at all in places predominantly male privileged.

Examples of women-created spaces, from the 1970s into the 1990s, abound. Among them are the Women's Ordination Conferences, the Women Church movement,[21] WATER (the Women's Alliance for Theology, Ethics, and Ritual) and the Grail, all initiated by Roman Catholic women; the Re-Imagining Conferences[22] and the Women's Theological Center, initiated predominantly by Protestant women; together with various Jewish women's groups.[23] Such spaces appear locally as well as nationally.

But the separate spaces being created by women today are distinct from those of the nineteenth century, and also those of the 1970s, in at least three regards. First, today's spaces are not as marginal to so-called mainline religious institutions as were the societies of the nineteenth century or the organizations of the 1970s. Today's spaces are instead spaces into and out of which women move. Boundaries between women-created spaces and traditional male privileged spaces are more permeable. Women, as noted above, are more likely to wander in and out of these variously configured spaces, patching together a fabric of faith and life sturdy enough to sustain our struggle for a new reality.

Second, today's separate spaces are, more than those of the past, often centred upon women's own religious rituals and committed to women's articulation of our own religious thoughts. These spaces are thereby responding to the growing recognition that traditional, male-created religious imagery, practices and discourses reinforce, indeed sacralize, social attitudes, behaviours and structures that privilege men and relegate women to a derivative, often violating, social as well as religious status.[24] In this sense, many women-created spaces today are spaces in which the horizon of the new reality for which we hope is brought nearer through the religious affirmation of women's presence and full participation as creators of images and rituals and discourses reflective of our own image as the divine image.[25]

Finally, many of today's women-created spaces are distinguished by women's willingness to wrestle honestly with the difficulties of forming new coalitions and new communities. More than in the nineteenth century or in the 1970s, women see *both* the interconnectedness of structures of oppression (racial, cultural, sexual, class, physical, etc.) *and* the intricate ways in which women are implicated in these structures, i.e., ways in which many of us are oppressors as well as oppressed. Here again ambivalence is heralded for our attention. This herald calls women to acknowledge conflictual alliances and concrete controversies among and between women, rather than simply to assume a 'sisterhood' that has no real referent or sustainable space.

Women are not only practising presence in spaces created for and by women. Women are also practising presence in public places of religious leadership. Here too, the very presence of women in the pulpits of Christian churches and Jewish synagogues and temples is at once a challenge to the tradition of male-only religious leadership and the affirmation of a new reality. Specifically, women's presence in public spaces of religious leadership challenges the centuries-long split between sexuality and spirituality, between body and mind, and affirms, indeed reveals, the wholeness of all human beings. Women's presence is so radically efficacious because, in the words of Elaine Lawless, women in spaces of public religious leadership blow the cover on 'the myth of the asexual minister'.[26] When people see women – whom Western cultural and religious traditions have identified and imaged as bodies and, accordingly, as sexual beings, in contrast to rational, spiritual men – in a public place of religious leadership, they are no longer able to see the male rabbi, priest or pastor as asexual. Suddenly, in the presence of women in public religious leadership, people are confronted so forcefully with what has been an assumed incongruity of sexuality and religiosity that previous assumptions are for ever shaken. At the least, previous assumptions will need to be reasserted with a repressive forcefulness not necessary heretofore.

An event that makes the efficacy of women's public presence explicit took place a year ago in Oakland, California. On a Sunday in the fall of 1997, nearly 300 people gathered at Oakland's Bishop Begin Plaza. Most were women, among them were a number of women who had been members of the Grail for five or six decades. About a third of those present were men. Most were Catholic, but Baptists, Jews, and members of the United Church of Christ were also present. Some who gathered were homeless women and men who regularly inhabit the plaza. This motley congregation was there to celebrate 'a Critical Mass'.

According to Jane Redmont's Special to the *National Catholic Reporter*:

Bright banners, flags, and stoles flapped in the wind. The liturgy made strong use of the arts – fabric, dance, music, theatre. Until the blessing of the gifts, it was an alternating movement between a traditionally vested male priest – a married priest – and a new way of celebrating, a circle of blessing led by women. The Eucharist we will create together today, said one of the organizers in the opening statement, is the Mass as we know it with a Mass that we can only begin to imagine . . . We are claiming the freedom in our church to try on, to experiment and to do so publicly.[27]

Redmont further reflected:

In many ways, this celebration is nothing new. Catholic women – and in some cases groups of women and men, often with children among them – have been celebrating the Eucharist together for at least a decade, in some cases longer. What we do here today, one of the organizers says at the beginning, calls other Roman Catholic women across our nation and globe to do publicly what we have for years done privately . . . Some of us do experience a call to priestly ministry. We endeavour to study, discern and practice its liturgical, pastoral and administrative dimensions – administration in the sense of helping the local church to put into practice its gifts, both internally and at the service of a hungry world. Most of all – and a Critical Mass reflects this – we care about bodies: all the baptized and the body to which they belong, the body as a whole in its unity and diversity.[28]

Having represented a Critical Mass as a liturgy of bodies – 'I understand the body of Christ in a way I had not before . . . You are my flesh and blood, we are saying, and Christ's flesh and blood. We know this in the breaking of the bread and the sharing of the cup; we know this in touching each others' bodies' – Redmont makes the connection to the crucial question: 'Does the ordination discussion come down, fundamentally, to bodies – women's bodies? Born into a woman's body, I may not be ordained . . . If we truly honoured women's bodies, in this religion that sees God in human flesh, would ordination of women even be an issue?'[29]

Precisely! Therefore, women's presence – women's presence as women's bodies – in public places of religious leadership is a refusal of centuries of teaching denigration of our bodies and our sexuality. Women's presence as women's bodies is also courageous affirmation of a new reality: the wholeness of humanity for women and men in mind and body. Of course, this affirmation of a new reality is as theologically radical as it is anthropologically radical. Women's presence in public places of religious leadership, this is to say, reveals the deepest roots of Western cultural and religious fragmentation in monotheism's asexual, spiritual – and false – God. This revelation liberates women, and men, to live and flourish in a new reality. This revelation also liberates God, the living God, in whose image we are truly created to be co-creators.

IV. Present awakenings

It is not clear whether what has begun will come to fruition. As I write, here in Rochester, New York, a battle rages in the Corpus Christi parish, and throughout the Roman Catholic diocese, in the aftermath of the firing of a priest, Jim Callan, and later of the pastoral associate, Mary Ramerman. Three practices – eucharistic hospitality extended to all; blessings of gay and lesbian unions; a woman on the altar with half-stole during the celebration of the eucharist – have been noted as reasons for the removals. On the one hand, this battle is part of the war over 'women's place' being waged world-wide, of which I spoke at the outset. One Vatican official is quoted as having said of pastoral associates: 'Some of these women are well intentioned, but the bulk of them are power-hungry witches. They have no concern for the church and for souls.'[30] On the other hand, the presence of Mary Ramerman and Jim Callan in public places of religious leadership also confirms what a recent book argues: the pastoral and theological groundwork and framework for ordaining women as priests is already in place.[31] The book has already been banned by the Vatican.

It is not clear whether what has begun will come to fruition. Even as women are living into a new reality – crossing and criss-crossing boundaries, unleashing creative imagination – within Christian and Jewish traditions, women are also choosing to leave. Many women are finding their way into the feminist spirituality movement, which is, in the words of Cynthia Eller, 'an admixture of Jungianism, ecology, Native American religions, political feminism, paganism, Buddhism, Theosophy, and just about anything else you would care to list'.[32] But, contends Eller, this movement is not at all the 'hopeless junk heap'[33] it appears to be. 'I would submit,' she continues, 'that spiritual feminists *are* creating a new religion, and doing so in the time-honoured fashion of all religions . . . All religions, however established and illustrious they are, were once similarly constructed from older elements. Creating a religion is always a matter of rearranging existing religious forms, taking a new slant on old practices, perhaps introducing a new element or two from outside the common cultural storehouse.'[34]

I think that in all religious traditions this sort of rearranging, taking a new slant and introducing new elements from the culture, occurs not only at the outset: it is ongoing. Women in religious leadership are participating in this ongoing process, from multiple locations and positions. There is no doubt whether women will thereby transform the religious traditions we have known in the West. The question left unanswered is how, and to what extent, women will change Christianity and Judaism and even Islam.

There is no easy, certainly no obvious, answer to this question. But as I keep my eyes 'on the ground and the horizon simultaneously', I am convinced that women will continue to transgress boundary lines that have in these times become battle lines. I am convinced that therefore borders will be ever more blurred, walls more permeable, and that more than one way to walk into wholeness, both human and divine, will become apparent and actualized.

Notes

1. Hannah Nyala, *Point Last Seen: A Woman Tracker's Story*, Boston 1997, 6.
2. As I write, a headline from the festival in Harare, Zimbabwe, to mark the end of the Ecumenical Decade of the Churches in Solidarity with Women declares: 'Churches accused of ignoring or condoning violence against women', *Ecumenical News International*, 30 November 1998. The literature on women and violence with particular attention to the churches is growing. Among the growing number of books on the churches and violence against women, see Aruna Gnanadason, *No Longer a Secret: The Church and Violence against Women*, Geneva 1993, and Pamela Cooper-White, *The Cry of Tamar: Violence Against Women and the Church's Response*, Minneapolis 1995.
3. The literature on fundamentalism and gender is growing. See for example Margaret Lamberts Bendroth, *Fundamentalism and Gender: 1875 to the Present*, New Haven and London 1993; Betty A. DeBerg, *Ungodly Women: Gender and the First Wave of American Fundamentalism*, Minneapolis 1990; John Stratton Hawley (ed.), *Fundamentalism and Gender*, New York and Oxford 1994; Pamela S. Nadell, *Women Who Would Be Rabbis: A History of Women's Ordination 1889–1985*, Boston 1998.
4. See, for example, Edward C. Lehman, Jr, *Gender and Work: The Case of the Clergy*, Albany, NY 1993; Barbara Brown Zikmund, Adair T. Lummis and Patricia Mei Yin Chang, *Clergy Women: An Uphill Calling*, Louisville 1998.
5. See Mark Chaves, *Ordaining Women: Culture and Conflict in Religious Organizations*, Boston, Mass. 1997.
6. For example, several denominations in the United States have developed permanent, and ordained, diaconal ministry, which is predominantly female. Additionally, a second alternative ordination track, in which clergy are ordained to serve a single local parish only, is gaining momentum in the Episcopal Church (Canon 9 priesthood) and the United Methodist Church (licensed lay pastors). Already data suggest that women will be disproportionately disadvantaged by such a

two-tier ordination system. See Paula Nesbitt, *Feminization of the Clergy in America*, New York and Oxford 1997, esp. 115–23. See also Paula Nesbitt, 'Dual Ordination Tracks: Differential Benefits and Costs for Men and Women Clergy', in *Gender and Religion*, ed. W. H. Swatos, Jr, New Brunswick, 27–44.

7. See Paula Nesbitt, *Feminization of the Clergy in America* (n. 6), 135ff.

8. For a clear and compelling discussion of exclusion, see Miroslav Volf, *Exclusion and Embrace: A Theological Exploration of Identity, Otherness and Reconciliation*, Nashville 1996.

9. Zikmund, Lummis and Chang, *Women Clergy. An Uphill Calling* (n. 4), 22.

10. See, for example, Elisabeth Schüssler Fiorenza, *In Memory of Her: A Feminist Theological Reconstruction of Christian Origins*, New York and London 1983, and 'The Twelve and the Discipleship of Equals', in *Discipleship of Equals: A Critical Feminist Ekklesia-logy of Liberation*, New York and London 1993; Luise Schottroff, *Lydia's Impatient Sisters: A Feminist Social History of Early Christianity*, Louisville and London 1995; Luise Schottroff, 'Toward a Feminist Reconstruction of the History of Early Christianity', in Luise Schottroff, Silvia Schroer and Marie-Theres Wacker, *Feminist Interpretation: The Bible in Women's Perspective*, Minneapolis 1998.

11. See, for example, Ross Kraemer, *Her Share of the Blessings: Women's Religions among Pagans, Jews and Christians in the Greco-Roman World*, New York and Oxford 1992, and Anne Jensen, *God's Self-Confident Daughters: Early Christianity and the Liberation of Women*, Louisville 1996.

12. See, for example, Susan Hill Lindley, *'You Have Stept Out of Your Place': A History of Women and Religion in America*, Louisville 1996; Carl Schneider and Dorothy Schneider, *In Their Own Right: The History of American Clergywomen*, New York 1997. See also Rosemary Radford Ruether and Rosemary Skinner Keller (eds), *In Our Own Voices: Four Centuries of American Women's Religious Writings*, San Francisco 1995.

13. Catherine Wessinger (ed.), *Women's Leadership in Marginal Religions. Explorations Outside the Mainstream*, Urbana and Chicago 1993, 1.

14. See, for example, Zikmund, Lummis and Chang, *Women Clergy* (n. 4); Martha Long Ice, *Clergy Women and Their Worldviews: Calling for a New Age*, New York 1987; Ruth Wallace, *They Call Her Pastor*, Albany, NY 1992.

15. See Frederick W. Schmidt, Jr, *A Still Small Voice. Women, Ordination and the Church*, Syracuse, NY 1996. See also Paula Nesbitt, *The Feminization of the Clergy in America* (n. 6); Edward C. Lehman Jr, *Gender and Work: The Case of the Clergy* (n. 4), Mark Chaves, *Ordaining Women: Culture and Conflict in Religious Organizations* (n. 5); Catherine Wessinger (ed.), *Religious Institutions and Women's Leadership: New Roles inside the Mainstream*, Columbia, SC 1996, etc.

16. See, for example, The Berkshire Clergywomen and Allison Stokes, *Women Pastors*, New York 1995. See also June Steffensen Hagen (ed.), *Rattling Those Dry Bones: Women Changing the Church*, San Diego 1995.

17. See 'Survey reveals widespread prejudice against women priests', *Ecumenical News International*, 30 April 1998.

18. See Zikmund, Lummis and Chang, *Women Clergy* (n. 4), esp. 114ff.

19. See Miriam Therese Winter, Adair Lummis and Allison Stokes, *Defecting in Place. Women Claiming Responsibility for Their Own Spiritual Lives*, New York 1994.

20. For a sharply focussed, succinct discussion of 'woman's place' and public space in the nineteenth century, including the various movements and societies created by and for women, see Glenna Matthews, *The Rise of Public Woman: Woman's Power and Woman's Place in the United States 1630–1970*, New York and Oxford 1992, 93–146. See also Anne Firor Scott, *Natural Allies: Women's Associations in American History*, Urbana and Chicago 1991.

21. See Rosemary Radford Ruether, *Women-Church: Theology and Practice of Feminist Liturgical Communities*, New York 1985.

22. See Nancy J. Berneking and Pamela Carter Joern (eds), *Re-Membering and Re-Imagining*, Cleveland 1995.

23. The story of one group of Jewish women is beautifully told by E. M. Broner. See *The Telling: The Story of a Group of Jewish Women Who Journey to Spirituality Through Community and Ceremony*, San Francisco 1993. See also Rebecca Alpert, *Like Bread on the Seder Plate: Jewish Lesbians and the Transformation of Tradition*, New York 1997.

24. In Mary Daly's by now classic phrase that captures this precisely, 'If God is male, then male is God', *Beyond God the Father. Toward a Philosophy of Women's Liberation*, Boston 1973.

25. For recent documentation of one group of women's communities that centre upon celebration of the eucharist see Sheila Durkin Dierks, *WomenEucharist*, Boulder, Colo 1997, among others.

26. Elaine J. Lawless, *Holy Women, Wholly Women: Sharing Ministries Through Life Stories and Reciprocal Ethnography*, Philadelphia 1993, 30.

27. Jane Redmont, 'Women stake claim to rites', *National Catholic Reporter*, 17 October 1997.

28. Ibid.

29. Ibid. See also Louis-Marie Chauvet and François Kabasele Lumbala (eds), *Liturgy and the Body, Concilium* 1995/3.

30. Quoted in 'Not Doing as the Romans Do', *Time*, 30 November 1998, 8.

31. Lavinia Byrne, *Women at the Altar*, New York and London 1998.

32. Cynthia Eller, *Living in the Lap of the Goddess: The Feminist Spirituality Movement in America*, New York 1993, 38–9.

33. Ibid., 38.

34. Ibid., 39. See also Richard Grigg, *When God becomes Goddess. The Transformation of American Religion*, New York 1995.

'We Women Are Church': Roman Catholic Women Shaping Ministries and Theologies

Mary E. Hunt

Introduction

'We women are church' is the way an octogenarian Roman Catholic Swiss feminist greeted me at her door when we first met. She had heard me say those words on a radio programme in a discussion of what it means to be part of the women-church movement. She knew exactly what I meant. She was determined to live out her remaining years with the firm conviction that she, too, was church. Happily, she did.

Being church was a new concept for her, as it was for me, and for the thousands of other Roman Catholic women who affirm ourselves as 'church' despite the remarkable recalcitrance on the part of the kyriarchal institution to bring its structures and teachings in line with contemporary theological thought and spiritual practice. Why and how we do so is an important chapter in church history. It is the story of power transformed.

Twenty-five years after the first Women's Ordination Conference meeting (Detroit, Michigan, November 1975), theological attention is focussed on how Roman Catholic women are shaping the ministries and theologies of the community. Some Catholics note this innovation with a deep sense of panic because it means that firmly entrenched patterns of domination and exclusion are being challenged. Others, myself included, rejoice that we are finally asking the right questions. Now we can leave behind the divisive agenda that was set for women within patriarchal parameters – to be ordained or not to be ordained – and the unsatisfactory answers that arose from both options in favour of constructive alternatives that reflect shared power.

The many experiences, starting points and perspectives of Catholic women around the world make this new agenda one with plural expressions. This is a deliberate move away from perhaps the most oppressive aspect of patriarchal thinking, its insistence on one way of doing things, one model of church, one way of looking at questions. This multiplicity is our strength. This diversity is what it means to be 'catholic' in the new millenium. This is a shift in power dynamics.

In this article I will sketch how women are now shaping the ministerial and theological dimensions of twenty-first century Catholicism as part of an increasingly globalized inter-religious conversation. I do so from a starting point in the USA, where I work as an activist theologian in a community-based educational centre, the Women's Alliance for Theology, Ethics and Ritual (WATER). The very existence of WATER is due in some measure to the fact that neither Diann Neu, the other co-director, nor I, as progressive, theologically trained Catholic feminists, could find appropriate employment in kyriarchally controlled institutions. Like so many Catholic feminists, we simply set about doing what needs to be done, in our case, developing a centre where education, training, organizing and networking for ministry and theology take place. My perspective is clearly coloured by the US context, but it is also textured by significant interaction with colleagues in other parts of the world.

I. Feminist church history

Historians ponder how Catholicism shifted in the early centuries from a faith tradition in which women were involved to one in which women were marginalized, then nearly co-opted, and now exert important pastoral and intellectual energy. That history is complicated and contested, but it seems that rather than moving in a linear progression, each dynamic has been present throughout.

I pick up the story in the mid-twentieth century with Vatican II, when well-trained women, from both religious communities and beyond, were involved in informal discussions that influenced policy making.[1] Despite their inability to penetrate the provincial ways of thinking and operating that characterized a virtually all-male hierarchy, the Catholic community from the 1960s on has benefited from the considerable talents and insights of theologically trained women, whether these were welcome or not. This was part of the general spirit of openness and experimentation that prevailed in the conciliar and post-conciliar years. Catholic theology was seen as a vibrant science, a field where intellectual curiosity, commitment to social justice and spiritual search came together for women: finally, perhaps more so than for men.

Three factors made this change inevitable. First, women's educational levels, especially for women in religious congregations, rose dramatically in the post-war period in the West. The convent meant upward mobility for many Catholic women. The result was a cadre of well-educated women who could no longer be lied to or trivialized by clergy. Many women, not only nuns, entered seminaries and graduate programmes and began to prepare for theological and ministerial careers, training along-side and often surpassing male students.

Second, feminism and the women's movements exposed patriarchy as an oppressive system that conferred unearned privilege on some and denied access to opportunity to others. It was based on interstructured forms of domination, what Elisabeth Schüssler Fiorenza aptly termed 'kyriarchy', literally, structures of lordship, like racism, economic injustice, sexism and heterosexism.[2] Nowhere was this more obvious than in Catholicism. Everything from church architecture to the structures of decision-making, from the designs of the bishops' headgear to papal authority, was construed in a top-down way with virtually no horizontal lines.

Implicit in this culture, and often explicit in its teachings, was the radical inequality of men and women, of clergy and lay people, of adherents and those who do not believe, agree or act in the prescribed way. What was benignly characterized as 'difference' and attributed to 'nature' (as in women's special nature being an excuse to treat women in a second-class way) always meant discrimination, evidenced by the obligations and opportunities that accrued. For example, the opportunity to test one's priestly vocation was available only to men, with priesthood and decision-making restricted to celibate males. Feminist insistence on equality and commitment to justice simply undercut any essentialist notions of gender or class distinctions based on outmoded notions of nature. Thus an all-male priesthood is a contradiction in Christian theological terms, an insight most Christian churches came to long before Catholicism.

Third, this theological development came about thanks to the pion-eering feminist theological work of Catholic women including Mary Daly, Rosemary Radford Ruether and Elisabeth Schüssler Fiorenza.[3]

It is impossible to over-estimate the importance of their work in terms of its impact on Catholic theology. Though Mary Daly eventually left Catholicism, her mind-expanding linguistic forays and her signal insight that if God were father, then father was God, left an indelible mark on the field. Rosemary Radford Ruether's early study of the patristic period provided her with the tools to attempt her first foray into contemporary theology in favour of the use of contraceptives, followed by dozens of books on feminist church history and feminist systematic theology. Elisabeth Schüssler Fiorenza's early work on priesthood and later unparalleled biblical scholarship provided the scriptural grounding for feminist Catholic faith. She gave names to key concepts such as 'women-church', 'discipleship of equals', Jesus as 'Miriam's child and Sophia's prophet'. Joining with this trinity of talent, many Catholic feminist scholars built a firm intellectual foundation for moving women into ministry and theology as a logical consequence of this work.

These three factors – education, the feminist movement and, in particular, early Catholic feminist theological work – combined to lay the groundwork for the very successful ordination movement, successful in that women were not co-opted into a kyriarchal structure.

II. The success of the ordination movement

Women were ordained in most US Protestant denominations by the early 1970s. The stained-glass ceiling was definitively broken when eleven Episcopalian deacons were 'irregularly' ordained to the presbyterate in 1974 (the ordinations were 'regularized' by 1977). This achievement, together with ordination of Jewish women to the rabbinate (the first US woman rabbi was ordained by the Reform movement in 1972), fuelled interest and hope among Catholic women that it was just a matter of time, a brief time, before they, too, would be ordained. It was not to be so.

The Roman Catholic kyriarchy was in the unenviable position of having to defend an all-male presbyterate, with its dubious collapse of sacramental ministry and decision-making into one package, when the religious tide was moving rapidly in the other direction. In fact, in the thirty years since, virtually all of the other denominations have seen an extraordinary growth in the percentage of women in their ordained ranks, so that ministry is now an increasingly female profession in the US and in other parts of the world.

St Joan's Alliance, which began in England in 1911, was the earliest

Catholic group to raise the matter of women's ordination. Individual theologians wrote about the question, but it was not until the Detroit meeting in 1975, and the subsequent incorporation of the Women's Ordination Conference in 1976, that Catholic women in large numbers began to discuss ordination as a real option, albeit in deeply renewed forms. The Vatican's 1976 *Declaration on the Question of the Admission of Women to the Ministerial Priesthood* left little doubt about the virulence of the opposition when officials argued that the priesthood is not a right that can be given, but something that, in its gender-exclusive form based on Jesus' maleness, participates in 'the economy of the mystery of Christ and the Church'. The Vatican claimed that the teaching was unchangeable and the question was closed.

WOC responded with another conference in 1978 in Baltimore, Maryland, where optional celibacy, an end to clericalism, and the dismantling of hierarchy were discussed as conditions for women accepting priesthood. Ironically, the end of discussion for Rome was the beginning of a new kind of discussion for feminists, one in which the entire concept of priesthood and the current model of ecclesiology was up for review. Rather than responding defensively, women took the offensive by reframing the question from one primarily of gender to one of ecclesiology.

By the early 1980s, many feminist Catholics, scandalized by the Vatican's position and increasingly accustomed to women ministers and theologians, began to meet for sacrament and solidarity in local base communities. These groups in loose affiliation became known as the women-church movement, a global, ecumenical movement made up of local feminist base communities of justice-seekers who engage in sacrament and solidarity.[4] In the USA the movement is led by the Women-Church Convergence, a group of more than thirty 'autonomous Catholic-rooted organizations/groups raising a feminist voice and committed to an ekklesia of women which is participative, egalitarian and self-governing'.[5] The Convergence has sponsored three conferences: 'From Generation to Generation: Women-Church Speaks' (Chicago, Illinois 1983); 'Women-Church: Claiming Our Power' (Cincinnati, Ohio 1987) and 'Women-Church: Weavers of Change' (Albuquerque, New Mexico 1993), where thousands of adherents gathered as the 'ecclesia of women' to worship and shape commitments to social justice. The titles show a steady progression in the movement, from its initiation to claiming power to using that power to make change.

Hundreds of women-church groups grew up around the world –

Frauen Kirchen in Germany and Switzerland, *mujer iglesia* in Argentina and Uruguay – as many women, some men and quite a few children practised their Catholic faith, including the eucharist, in feminist base communities, without benefit of clergy. Communities simply relied on members to carry out the worship and engage in the diaconal tasks that are proper to baptized Christians. The movement crystallized the feminist resolve to 'be church' rather than simply to change the kyriarchal church, a prospect that looked increasingly unlikely.

As women-church has grown apace, so, too, has the influence of Catholic feminism on the larger Catholic community. Catholic renewal groups, especially the Catholics Organizing for Renewal and the International Movement We Are Church, coalitions in the USA and Europe respectively, have been affected by feminists, women and men, who affirm the 'discipleship of equals' approach as they go about the work of renewal of the structures and practices of kyriarchy. Many of them also worship in base communities, sometimes with married male priests presiding at the eucharist.

Meanwhile, many rank-and-file Catholics became accustomed to women ministering in, even pastoring, their parishes due to the shortage of male celibate priests and the generosity of the women. These women ministers came up against the limitations of not being ordained, namely, their inability to function fully in sacramental roles when pastoral needs demand, and the theological absurdity of working for an organization that prefers to preserve a celibate male priesthood at the expense of eucharistic community.

These two realities – the flourishing of clergy-free communities and the rise of women without ordination functioning as priests in parishes, universities, prisons, hospitals and hospices – fuel the conversation about women's ordination, shifting it eventually to a focus on the quality of ministry. How can small communities guarantee that they provide adequate pastoral resources for their members, and how can women who are ministering do so competently, given the limits placed on their roles? These are useful questions. They are not finally about ordination but about ministry, the quality of which is too often sacrificed in the quest to keep it all-male. Nonetheless, the arguments against the ordination of women were reiterated in a 1994 papal pronouncement, *Ordinatio sacerdotalis*, followed in 1995 by a *Responsum* clarifying that the teaching, while not infallible, requires religious obedience. To say that it does not receive such obedience would be to labour the point.

Undaunted, at its twentieth-anniversary gathering in 1995, WOC hosted an international assembly to carry on feminist conversations about renewed priestly ministry on the one hand, and about new forms of ecclesial life, namely women-church as a discipleship of equals, on the other. This healthy tension has been present in the movement and across regional boundaries for decades. Not all Catholic feminist women agree with one another about the shape of ministry and theology to come. But the triumph is that all women who engage in these conversations are, and respect the fact that others are, theological agents who can and must articulate their own insights. Women are setting a theological agenda and living it out together in all of its plurality, in sharp contrast to the one-answer approach that we learned.

I consider this to be the great success of the ordination movement. The Vatican cannot co-opt women who will not accept ordination to a clerical, celibate, hierarchical priesthood. Moreover, Catholic feminists are giving shape and life to alternative Catholic communities in which people live out their sacramental rights and their solidarity responsibilities despite the fact that Rome refuses to change its polity. Some might argue that I am making a virtue of necessity in this analysis, claiming success in the face of obvious failure to achieve ordination. That is to miss the point, unless ordination of women in a kyriarchal structure is the goal. Rather, more profound ministerial and theological changes have taken hold as the Catholic women who have 'defected in place' and those who have moved on form new communities and exercise their moral and theological agency.[6]

III. The shape of Catholic feminist ministry and theology

Catholic feminist ministry and theology take a variety of forms. Globalization means that the movements are not simply US-based, but international. Just as women-church is expressed variously in different countries, though thus far without formal international co-ordination, so too the agenda for women-centred change is finding expression in a range of contexts. In 1996, at the European Women's Synod in Gmunden, Austria, a group of Catholic women, spearheaded by the US Women's Ordination Conference, formed Women's Ordination Worldwide (WOW), a coalition of advocacy groups focussed on female priesthood. Members include the Maria von Magdala group from Germany, which presses for women's ordination as well as inclusive language in liturgy, and equal opportunity for women in recruitment for church-related positions, including theological faculties.

Other member groups with similar goals are Catholic Women's Ordination in England; Brothers and Sisters in Christ in Ireland; the Ordination of Catholic Women, Women and the Australian Church, and Women of the New Covenant, all in Australia; Catholic Women Knowing Our Place, New Zealand; Catholic Network for Women's Equality of Canada; Women's Ordination, South Africa; and a Spanish group called the Collective of Women in the Church. Nascent groups in India, Korea and the Czech Republic are also in contact, proving that the movement is indeed worldwide.[7] While each group has a commitment to the ordination of women in some form, the majority of them make clear their concern for larger issues of inclusivity and their collaboration with other reform groups such as those working for optional celibacy for male priests.

In addition to this advocacy work, the biggest changes brought about by Catholic feminists are taking place in pastoral practice. Reliable statistics are not available for many countries; Rome has perhaps not seen fit to measure what it wishes would go away. But in those places where numbers are available, the trend towards ministry becoming a predominantly female profession is clear. In the USA, for example, more than 10% of Catholic parishes do not have a resident priest. Women now pastor many parishes with apparent success, and are received warmly.[8] I take this as evidence that ordination is not necessary for the pastoral role, inviting theological speculation about just what ordination might mean sacramentally in a church that approximates to a 'discipleship of equals'. That remains to be articulated.

In the USA, women make up 82% of the estimated 26,000 parish ministers who are not priests.[9] Reasons for this include generally low pay, long hours, high expectations of nurture and the low prestige associated with current models of ministry, especially religious education. This recipe for a female job in a patriarchal culture is increasingly less attractive to men, as evidenced by the nearly 40% decrease in the number of ordained male priests from 1965 to (projected) 2005.[10] Nonetheless, it seems clear that in the twenty-first century, Catholic women will do for churches what they did for Catholic educational and medical establishments in the nineteenth and twentieth centuries, that is, provide high-quality service with low-quality reward.

Theological schools are already feeling the effects of women's entrance into ministry. Many Catholic seminaries are now dependent on women students in degree programmes to keep their doors open, despite the fact that placement offices in the seminaries have not been aggressive in addressing gender oppression against their alumnae. Graduate programmes in religion at non-Catholic institutions report Catholic women and men in numbers approaching parity.

However, two factors converge to leave in question the impact of these phenomena. First, increased religious pluralism means that Roman Catholic feminists have many opportunities for ordained ministry in other denominations that treat women fairly and pay them a just wage for their work. There has not been a mass exodus in this direction, but there is enough crossover to leaven the Catholic community with women who, while ordained in other denominations, continue to maintain their Catholic identity. In fact they can be thought of as 'Catholic priests' after a fashion. Women seem to have little trouble holding together such seeming contradictions, with the predictable result that what it means to call oneself Catholic continues to expand, thanks to feminist Catholics' creativity.

Second, many Catholic feminists have found so problematic the theology that oppresses women, and so helpful the spiritual resources from other traditions that contain no such contradictions (for example, Zen meditation and certain Celtic practices), that they have expanded their own spiritual repertoires to include these. Once again, they do not become 'less Catholic' as a result, but 'Catholics' who are more in tune with the pluralistic religious times in which we live. I predict that this syncretism in the most positive sense of the word will have increasing influence on the shape of Catholic feminist ministry and theology. It foreshadows a time when Catholics in general will appreciate their faith as part of a multi-religious mix.

Coupled with this spiritual expansion is the constricting conservatism in Catholic educational institutions, which threatens their academic future. The impact of the Vatican's 1990 *Ex corde Ecclesiae* portends severe restrictions on theologians in that they will be required to be licensed by the kyriarchy in order to teach in Catholic universities. The result of this policy, already in place as a matter of practice if not a matter of law in many schools, will be the erasure of feminists from the faculties. The next generation of students will not have the benefit of feminist professors in the classroom and the supervision of feminists for their dissertations, a threat to the future of Catholic feminist thought. This is already the case in many Catholic theological faculties in Europe, the USA and Latin America, where the purge of feminists whose doctrinal views do not conform to the kyriarchal views is decimating the ranks.[11]

In many respects, the matter of ordaining women is one of the tamest of theological differences between Catholic feminists and the kyriarchy. In addition to the new sources mentioned above, ethical matters – such as the moral importance of safe sex including the use of condoms, effective birth control as a normative part of responsible reproduction, abortion as an always difficult but sometimes necessary choice, same-sex relations on a moral par with heterosexual relations – tend to provoke more dissonance.

Feminist ecumenical approaches such as shared eucharist with Protestants, the recognition of salvation beyond Christian parameters, and the welcome engagement in inter-religious dialogue as constitutive aspects of Catholic feminist theological practice point to a certain eclipsing of kyriarchal patterns. In each instance, what is in play is not only a new practice, but, of greater importance, evidence of a new sense of shared power. No longer must Catholics be 'right' to be spiritual, nor must Catholics guard their bread and wine from those whose interpretations of eucharist are not precisely the same. Rather, feminists have brought a new sense of openness, a new sense of hospitality, born of having suffered the lack of it at home. These changes result in a broader sharing of power, a deeper recognition that diversity is, finally, catholic.

IV. What to expect

The question remains: If we women are church, what kind of church are we women? This is not so much a query about the shape of the institution or the gender of its ministers as one of power. It is really the question of who will decide what kind of church we will bequeath to our children. This is where the most serious struggles are yet to unfold. The silencing of feminist theologians like Ivone Gebara of Brazil is only the beginning.

Three major power issues stand out as women continue to gain ground as religious agents, protagonists of their own spirituality. First, the very word Catholic remains contested. To whom is this identifier linked? Is it simply to the kyriarchal church, or does the term properly belong to all those baptized people who profess a commitment to sacrament and solidarity in continuity with the Jesus movement, as progressive feminists would contend?

An oft-used strategy by religious conservatives is to say that Catholic feminist approaches to ministry and theology are all well and good in themselves, but that they are not 'Catholic' because they do not conform to the kyriarchal model. No longer is this so easy to do. Catholic feminists respond that our models of ministry and theological views are nothing but Catholic, linked to the early Jesus movement, consistent with gospel values, and agreed to by millions of people who identify as Catholic. If anything, it is the Vatican's view that seems out of step with the consistent tradition, though most Catholic feminists see no need to mimic their strategy and proclaim the Vatican not Catholic. Perhaps we should; however, this is not a legal wrangle over a trademark, but rather a theological debate about whether one or many possibilities exist. More important, it is a debate over who can claim the title Catholic and all that accompanies it, especially who has access to and control over the resources – both material and human – that have accrued over centuries in the name of the whole community.

Second, flowing from this is the ability to act in the name of the Catholic community, which has implications in the legal and policy arenas. From witnessing marriages to influencing legislation, 'Catholic' has clout. For example, Catholic women ministers in the USA are not ordained, therefore they are not licensed to witness marriages. Their confessional seal is not protected by law. They do not benefit from clergy tax laws, as do their ordained counterparts in other traditions. This will need to change.

The policy arena is even more contested. Government officials are gradually realizing that the kyriarchal church is not all there is to Catholicism. For example, at the UN International Conference on Population and Development in Cairo in 1994, the Vatican met its feminist match when it enlisted some fundamentalist Muslims to join it in opposing the popular platform of action that included birth control and abortion. Catholics for a Free Choice, a feminist group based in Washington, DC, led the opposition. A lack of basic diplomatic courtesy on the part of Vatican officials, and their insistence on thinking and behaving as they are accustomed to doing in their own setting, where women are scarce, did not play well in Cairo. What was significant was that people around the world understood that this was Catholics arguing with Catholics, and that the kyriarchy was not the exclusive Catholic voice. CFFC went on to raise serious questions about the Vatican as a city-state, a religious group as a government with a voice at such meetings. These challenges to hegemonic religious power that has spilled over into the public policy arena are, I predict, Catholic feminists' deepest inroads into new power arrangements.

Third, the question of ordination remains unresolved, not so much over the matter of gender, which now seems obvious, as over the matter of linking ordination and decision-making. The sacramental function of presiding at a eucharist is one thing, but making decisions about everything from the use of funds to recruiting professors is where another kind of power resides. Ordaining a few women to join a few men who, because of their ordination, automatically are those who have authority and jurisdiction in these arenas, pales before the wholesale change needed in the models of Catholic community governance.

'Discipleship of equals' is as much a political as a theological concept, based on radical democracy and participation.[12] Women-church groups struggle with how to share leadership as well as function efficiently, how to empower all members but not disempower those who do the work. Church reform groups struggle to find ways to bring the community together in an assembly of the whole, the ekklesia. Canonical religious communities influenced by feminism struggle with how to move their financial resources from kyriarchal control to community control. Progressive parishes struggle with how to implement the ministerial and theological changes they want and still maintain their tie to the kyriarchy.

As they unfold, these struggles and others to come will reveal just how far the paradigm has shifted, in fact, how much influence feminist thought and action has had on what was once thought to be a monolithic tradition.[13] Now, when I say, 'We women are church', I am confident that many people, like my Swiss friend, take themselves and me very seriously.

Notes

1. Carmel McEnroy set the record straight on the participation of women at Vatican II in *Guests in Their Own House: The Women of Vatican II*, New York 1996. Patty Crowley's story of attempting to bring the experience of heterosexually married Catholics to the birth control debate conducted by male celibates is in Robert McClory, *Turning Point: The Inside Story of the Papal Birth Control Commission and How Humanae Vitae Changed the Life of Patty Crowley and the Future of the Church*, New York 1995.

2. Elisabeth Schüssler Fiorenza, *But She Said: Feminist Practices of Biblical Interpretation*, Boston 1992, 8.

3. Their early work included: Mary Daly. *The Church and the Second Sex*, Boston 1968, and her classic *Beyond God the Father: Toward a Philosophy of Women's Liberation*, Boston 1973; Rosemary Radford Ruether, *The Radical Kingdom: The Western Experience of Messianic Hope*, New York 1970 and her pioneering *Sexism and God-Talk: Toward a Feminist Theology*, Boston and London 1983; Elisabeth Schüssler Fiorenza, *Der vergessene Partner: Grundlagen, Tatsachen und Möglichkeiten*

der beruflichen Mitarbeit der Frau in der Heilssorge der Kirche, Düsseldorf 1964, and her groundbreaking *In Memory of Her: Feminist Theological Reconstruction of Christian Origins*, New York and London 1983.

4. For the original concept of women-church, see Elisabeth Schüssler Fiorenza's Epilogue, 'Toward A Feminist Biblical Spirituality: The Ekklesia of Women', in *In Memory of Her* (n. 3). For some of the history, see Rosemary Radford Ruether *Women-Church: Theology and Practice*, San Francisco 1985. For an overview of the theology and liturgy, see Mary E. Hunt and Diann L. Neu, *Women-Church Sourcebook*, Silver Spring, MD 1993.

5. Women-Church Convergence brochure, 1999.

6. See Miriam Therese Winter, Adair Lummis and Allison Stokes, *Defecting in Place: Women Claiming Responsibility for Their Own Spiritual Lives*, New York 1994.

7. Information on Women's Ordination Worldwide and the contemporary state of the movement was graciously provided by Andrea Johnson, National Coordinator of the Women's Ordination Conference in the United States.

8. Ruth A. Wallace, *They Call Her Pastor: A New Role for Catholic Women*, Albany, NY 1992.

9. The Notre Dame Study of Catholic Parish Life reports that over 80% of CCD teachers and catechumen sponsors are women; over 75% of those who lead adult Bible studies or discussion groups are women; over 85% of those who carry out traditional diaconal tasks (for example, visiting the sick, ministering to those who are handicapped) are women. David C. Leege and Thomas A. Trozzolo, 'Who Participates in Local Church Communities?', Notre Dame Study of Catholic Parish Life, *Origins* 15, 13 June 1985, 50–7 as cited in *Defecting in Place* (n. 6), 283.

10. Richard A. Schoenherr and Lawrence A. Young with Tsan-Yuang Cheng, *Full Pews, Empty Altars: Demographics of the Priest Shortage in the United States Dioceses*, Madison, WI 1993.

11. One notorious case in the US was that of Professor Carmel McEnroy, who was dismissed from her tenured position at St Meinrad Seminary. Not coincidentally, she is the author of a critical study of the role of Catholic women at the Second Vatican Council cited above.

12. See Elisabeth Schüssler Fiorenza, *Discipleship of Equals: A Critical Feminist Ekklesia-logy of Liberation*, New York and London 1993, as well as her earlier *Bread Not Stone: The Challenge of Feminist Biblical Interpretation*, Boston 1984, where she lays some of the groundwork.

13. See Maureen Fiedler and Linda Rabben (eds), *Rome Has Spoken . . . A Guide to Forgotten Papal Statements and How They Have Changed through the Centuries*, New York 1998.

IV · Concluding Reflection

The Authority of Women and the Future of the Church

Hermann Häring

I. Renewal without fixation (a summary)

This issue has not been discussing a particularly enjoyable topic. It was sparked off by a Roman document on the ordination of women, at most three pages long, which on its appearance caused perplexity and great indignation. As we can see, the document itself is having a peculiarly sterile effect. It can only forbid: it repeats what has already been said and in a subsequent declaration is endowed with the utmost authority, which makes the substantive question the question of obedience.[1] Heightened opposition has been the result; there is no point in tackling the document itself, since it contains no argument and no counter-argument that has not already been exchanged. I personally have been preoccupied with the question at the latest since 1971, when in his book *Why Priests?* Hans Küng stated: 'The church's ministry must not be exclusively male: it must not be an alliance of males. A properly renewed church today will include the full participation of women in the life of the church on the basis of equal rights.' So women too are to be ordained to a ministry the gradual sacralization of which needs to be thought about.[2] Since then the Roman tone of demand and repudiation has changed little; at most it has become sharper, has been reduced to some core statements and has gained disciplinary decisiveness. Moreover today the prohibition against the ordination of women has been included in the stream of general hardening: one need think only of the disturbing document *Ad Tuendam fidem*, which today is causing some theologians, men and women, sleepless nights.[3] Certainly Rome has not been able to implement the prohibition against discussion stated in *Ordinatio sacerdotalis* and endorsed by

Ratzinger,[4] but the question of ordination has meanwhile become a shibboleth, which has been decisive in the appointment of women to service in theology and the church, has caused unexpected difficulties to others, and led to yet others being removed from their functions.

The manifold reactions that this repressive document has nevertheless provoked are all the more amazing.[5] It has led to many clarifications. In many countries, theologians, both men and women, have usually declared their solidarity.[6] Here sufficient work had been done on the biblical evidence. Thus it was clear from the beginning that the question put to the Bible ('Did Jesus ordain women as priests?') was anachronistic and therefore meaningless. On the other hand, at an early stage people had become aware of another fact: there were cultural reasons for the astonishing absence of women in the practice of ministry of early Christianity, the covering of their traces and the concentration of males in holding office. At the same time, and despite everything, many traces were found of women who played an important role as apostles, leaders of (house) communities, or as prophetesses. Finally, as several articles show, Elisabeth Schüssler Fiorenza achieved a breakthrough with her manifold researches into the presence and absence of women, supported by hermeneutics and ideology criticism.[7] These made it clear that the question of Christian women in the church's ministry cannot be treated in isolation, but has to be understood as the result of a far-reaching process of inculturation. The important thing was therefore to discover the traces of an original conception, according to which the church is in principle and consistently to be understood as an 'Ekklesia of equals', as a church of women which does not exclude men (and therefore does not recompense evil with evil).

Here the old baptismal formula in Gal. 3.28 plays a central and normative role, against which even the present magisterium has only weak arguments: 'There is no longer Jew and Greek, slave and free, male and female.' Certainly there is quickly a fall from the level of this baptismal confession; after the Greek and the slave the woman gets forgotten (I Cor. 1.23; Col. 3.11). But in the light of many original traces, later developments can be described as ways to the patriarchate, to the un-Christian exclusion of women and thus to the church's halving of itself, even though it understands itself as the ark of all humankind. However, this way did not run as directly as is generally thought. Anne Jensen, for example, in her investigations of the early church, reports on 'mothers' of communities and women martyrs, prominent female figures and women representatives of Christ, prophetesses with quite sacramental functions. Evidently egalitarian models of the church persisted for a long time – though of course on small islands.[8]

There is also much to report about the history of women in the era after Constantine, including the Middle Ages and modernity.[9] Feminine power and creativity showed itself in many prominent figures, but these found their roles more in convents and in theological writing,[10] in social involvement or in a withdrawal into mysticism, and less in political activity, though for a long time the office of abbess was still held in high respect, sometimes given great authority, even over clergy, and could perform church functions to the verge of sacramental activity. Thus down to the twentieth century, supporters of the ordination of women remained, albeit in a dwindling minority. By contrast, theologians and the guardians of church order had adequate time to build up a tradition the result of which is brought out today by the church's magisterium: 'Excuse me, but what women want today has never existed! These innovations smack of revolution.' Now some remarks have already been made above about the problems of the church's magisterium. As has become evident, in past years the discussion has remained rooted in very formal questions: an attempt has been made to demonstrate that the Roman teaching is not infallible. However, it is time to subject the construction of infallibility itself to a critical revision, since the last great controversy has produced no answers. Here it could easily be shown that the claim to infallibility, understood as a comprehensive reality in the church, is itself the fruit of patriarchal elitist thinking. It merely forms the core of a very authoritarian, absolutist, completely un-Christian structure. Gómez Acebo has brought out only one aspect of this, namely the disastrous history of silence and silencing. A church of equals is hardly compatible with this praxis.

Nevertheless, some cheerful things can also be reported at the end of this issue. The first articles have shown how the discussion with Rome has been carried on with backward looks. Other articles, above all those by May, Hunt and Meyer Wilmes, however, make it clear that feminist theologians in particular have long since freed themselves from existing limits. Many of them no longer claim old rights but are trying out new ways in theory and praxis.[11] Rome regards the ordination of women as not only impermissible but also invalid: that is emphatically repudiated. But many women theologians also make it clear that those who do not rise above this conflict are merely repeating Roman thought and insisting only on a hardening, which is good neither for the church as a whole or for the women concerned. Those who insist only on receiving similar ordination are ultimately stabilizing a system which in the end has excluded women.[12] That is the reason why many women no longer aim at the ministry in its present form. They have long since renewed it in spirit and practice. They are no longer ready to tie their celebration of the eucharist, their proclamation of the Word, their prayer and their mutual help to a way of thinking in terms of a dominating authority, which surrounds itself with the insignia of old Roman power and limits collaboration with the communities to a well-controlled minimum.

Therefore the resistance to exclusion leads directly to reflection on new forms of participation, communication, diaconal action and church leadership. The aim is a creative transformation of church structures of ministry in all controversies. It might be mentioned in passing that – as we see above all in the United States – yet a further dimension is bound up with this. This is the rediscovery of religious leadership from an ecumenical and inter-religious perspective. Precisely because they had been marginalized for so long, women today offer better presuppositions for aiming at such breakthroughs for the well-being of the whole church.

II. An offer to the church (five theses)

But what are the conclusions to be drawn at the end of this issue? To end with, let me mention five aspects.

---

1. Signs of the time
The demand for the ordination of women is not the expression of an arbitrary self-assertiveness but the symptom of a far-reaching cultural revolution. It results in the call for a contemporary reform of the church.

The growing emancipation of women and criticism of their social situation in almost all cultures of our time has not left theology and the church untouched. Thus the question of women in the church's ministry was mentioned as early as 1948 in the First General Assembly of the World Council of Churches.[13] Step by step, in the following decades it has overrun the non-Catholic (Reformed and Free) churches and – at the latest in the 1960s – also reached the Catholic churches. The course of the discussion, from initial repudiation to positive solutions, has been repeated time and again. So far none of the churches involved has yet come to grief on the question. Nor have ecumenical relations between the churches suffered from it. On the contrary, as soon as the new experience has become established it has proved a blessing. That also applies to the decisions of the Anglican Church. Here all the discussions show with growing intensity that the issue is not just legal regulations but also the Christian form and credibility of the churches, the quality of their brotherliness and sisterliness, the respect and self-respect of women and other marginalized groups. In the face of the present symbolistic argument from Rome, the exclusion of women in particular has meanwhile become the symbol of an androcentric behaviour obsessed with domination. For this reason alone a protest needs to be made in the name of a 'church in today's world'. By the global criterion of cultural developments, the present refusal by the Catholic Church has the choice of recognizing the signs of the time or encouraging an enclosed subculture the sense of which is increasingly no longer understood – inside and outside the community of faith.

---

2. Inculturation and ideology criticism

The discussion of the acceptance or the prohibition of the ordination of women is a prime example of the usefulness of and need for contextual and emancipatory theologies.

The Roman documents have limited the discussion to two aspects: the ordination of women by Jesus and the fact that Jesus was a man. The first argument is anachronistic, and the second biologistic. Both arguments bear witness to an arbitrariness and randomness in which Rome's own prejudices are always demonstrated, since these arguments do not touch on the core statements of the Christian faith. By contrast, the standards of present-day Catholic theology include the discovery that faith is always inculturated faith. In faith, too, statements are always governed by cultural and social prejudices. Now the marginalization of women can be clearly recognized and identified as the consequence of cultural and social conditions. Those who nevertheless want to demonstrate that it is a central and indispensable element of Christian faith bear a hopeless burden of proof. Catholic theology cannot go on closing its eyes to the fact that any statement, argument or conclusion is ultimately governed by basic decisions ('fundamental options') and interests: ideology criticism is concerned with these. Therefore the basic interest of Christian faith also needs to be taken into consideration. This can be described in terms like 'humanization', 'justice', 'peace', 'liberation', 'reconciliation', 'brotherliness and sisterliness'. Christians who have recognized this cannot any longer accept any argument or practice in the Christian church which leads to splits or to the privileging of individual groups, including men. That forms the starting point for all contemporary emancipatory theologies.

---

3. Unconditional obligation
The obligation to do away with all injustice to women in the church is indivisible and unconditional.

However, the first and second theses must not lead to the exploitation of the question of women's ordination for general (inter-cultural or contextual) considerations. There is a widely accepted Christian conviction that the exclusion of women from leadership functions in the church is intrinsically unjust. It stands in intolerable contradiction to a Christian image of humankind. We should recall the great biblical metaphor that the human being (as woman or as man) is in the image of God, and the core Christian convictions that in baptism the difference between man and woman is overcome, and not just symbolically transcended (Gal. 3.28), that women too had or have a share in the 'universal priesthood', in the gifts of the spirit, in the tasks of church leadership, teaching, prophecy and diaconia; that in martyrdom men and women equally have been and are representatives of God. Therefore the prohibition against the ordination of women directly affects their unquenchable Christian dignity, unconditionally and regardless of any cultural, social or similar factors.

---

4. Reform and transformation
The discussion on the ordination of women is to be understood as a contribution to the reform and transformation of church structures.

'The ordination of women' has come to represent many complex problems. Only a few perspectives will be mentioned here. The issues are the right of women:

1. To represent churches or church communities both inside and outside those communities;
2. To take on functions of leadership and qualified decision-making;

3. To preside at the celebration of the eucharist and to oversee the ministry of other sacraments;
   There need to be new discussions of:
4. The connection between ministry and sacrament;
5. Institution to this ministry 'from above' (hierarchically) or 'from below' (by virtue of election by a community of the baptized);
6. The question of permanent control.
   But there are also the questions:
7. How the traditional ministries – of leadership and diakonia – are to be restructured;
8. By what criteria or content they are to be measured; and,
9. On what ecclesiastical, generally religious or social tasks they are to be orientated.

Above all it is necessary to investigate the false forms to which the exclusion of women hitherto has led. Women theologians in particular have developed models of this. Therefore it is quite clear that the present discussion also has a tremendous opportunity. It is one of reform and transformation. The specific experiences of women who had been excluded for centuries can now be discussed theoretically and introduced practically into the reality of the church.

---

5. An offer to the church
The call for the ordination of women serves the wellbeing and the future of the church.

The present discussion is strongly governed by Roman documents. Therefore it has to be maintained explicitly against 'Rome' that those who defend the ordination of women are not engaged in any battle against Rome, against church teaching or against particular church groups, but are concerned with the future viability of the church. They have something to offer: they are convinced that only a church of brothers and sisters can take up and withstand the challenge to our future with its manifold threats. So the present discussion also offers a tremendous chance to recognize the scope of the problem and see the opportunities for the future. It is highly desirable for the Catholic Church to recognize these signs of the time. This would be a blessing for it; it would get the ecumenical dialogue going again and open up unsuspected reserves in the worldwide battle for the rights, the liberation and the dignity of women. That must be worth any theoretical, practical and spiritual action, also on the part of the present church government.

Translated by John Bowden

Notes

1. W. Gross in W. Gross (ed.), *Frauenordination. Stand der Diskussion in der katholischen Kirche*, Munich 1996, 7.
2. H. Küng, *Why Priests?*, London 1972. This proposal is then taken up in *Reform und Anerkennung kirchlichen Ämter. Ein Memorandum der Arbeitsgemeinschaft ökumenischer Universitätsinstitute*, Munich and Mainz 1973, 22f. (thesis 20d), 174f.
3. One example of this is the English theologian John Wijngaards, who on 17 September 1998 formally resigned his priesthood and gave his reasons to the English press (cf. *The Tablet*, 19 September 1998, 1232).
4. Through my own personal activity I know only four cases of women who are at present having to defend themselves to their bishops or other church officials without the public being aware of this.
5. For the German-speaking world see Gross (ed.), *Frauenordination* (n. 1).
6. The church press in particular has taken up the question. Thus in the German-speaking world there is extensive documentation over recent years in *Herder-Korrespondenz*. In Great Britain an ongoing treatment of the topic can be found in *The Tablet*, which also takes into account developments in the Anglican Church. Finally the Internet offers rich and amazingly varied information about the discussion in all continents, including Asian countries and Australia.
7. Recently, Elisabeth Schüssler Fiorenza, 'Neutestamentlich-frühchristliche Arugmente zum Thema Frau and Amt. Eine kritische feministische Reflexion', in Gross (ed.), *Frauenordination* (n. 1), 32–44. This lists the early studies and articles and other studies relevant to the question.
8. Anne Jensen, *Gottes selbstbewusste Töchter. Frauenemanzipation im frühen Christentum?*, Freiburg 1992.
9. Some remarks on e.g. John Chystostom and Bonaventure can be found in P. Hünermann, 'Lehramtliche Dokumente zur Frauenordination', in Gross (ed.), *Frauenordination* (n. 1), 83–96, esp. 87f., cf. his article in *Theologische Quartalschrift* 173, 1993, 205–18.
10. See the 'Archiv für philosophie- und theologiegeschichtliche Frauen-forschung', founded in 1984 by Elisabeth Gössmann.
11. The progress in the discussion can easily be seen if one compares the early work of Ida Raming with discussions from the 1990s in which, in a renewed church, the priesthood no longer looks to be intrinsically desirable: I. Raming, *Der Ausschluss der Frau vom priesterlichen Amt – Gottgewollte Tradition oder Diskriminierung?*, Cologne 1973.
12. In the German-speaking world a more recent publication is evidence of this: Marianne Bühler, Brigitte Enzner-Probst, Hedwig Meyer-Wilmes and Hannelies

Steichele, *Frauen zwischen Dienst und Amt. Frauenmacht und –ohmacht in der Kirche. Beiträge zur Auseinandersetzung*, Düsseldorf 1998.

13. For the ecumenical situation see J. Field-Bibb, *Women towards Priesthood. Ministerial Politics and Feminist Praxis*, Cambridge 1991; for what follows see A. Jensen, 'Frauenordination und ökumenischer Dialog', in Gross (ed.), *Frauenordination* (n. 1), 100–5.

Dossier: The Practice of Ordaining Women in the Present Church

Theological Preparation and Establishment of the Ordination of Women in the Clandestine Church in Czechoslovakia

Petr Fiala and Jiří Hanuś

The discussion going on today within the Roman Catholic Church in many countries about the position of women in the church and the possibilities of their ordination predominantly concentrates on the theological, sociological and psychological aspects of the problem. Debate very often assumes a theoretical character. In this article we would like to draw attention to the fact that the Roman Catholic Church has already gained some practical experience in ordaining women: in Czechoslovakia, several women were ordained by the clandestine bishop Felix M. Davidek (1921–1988) in the first half of the 1970s within Koinotes, the unofficial ecclesiastical organization which he founded. This community was established under Davidek's supervision after his return from a Communist prison in the late 1960s with the aim of performing illegally those functions of the church that the Communist regime banned from official practice. In response to the Soviet invasion of Czechoslovakia in August 1968, when there was a threat of increased prosecution of the church by the Communist regime, Davidek, who was ordained bishop in 1967, started an alternative organization with secretly consecrated bishops and priests and a carefully worked out system of theological, philosophical and historical education. Gradually he developed widespread pastoral activities over the whole territory of Czechoslovakia, especially in Moravia.

Inside Koinotes, new forms of ecclesiastical life (one of the most debated being the ordination of married men) began to develop, influenced not only by the thoughts of Vatican II and the work of Teilhard de Chardin but also by Davidek's original approaches. Recently the information about Davidek's ordination of women has also been confirmed. The present results of our investigation into the history of the hidden church enable us to reconstruct (or at least to give a general outline of) the genesis of the tradition of women in this part of the hidden church and to point to some problems connected with this practice.[1]

The solution to the question of the ordination of women was related to an important turning-point in the activities of the Koinotes community that occurred at the end of 1970. Davidek called a Pastoral Synod on Christmas Day devoted to the problem of the development of the local church and especially to the position of women in the church. The decision to call the Synod was the result of a sudden impulse, because as Davidek later stated himself, it happened within six weeks. However, he had already busied himself with these topics for several years. He thought that the conditions in which the Koinotes community had been working until that time created an urgent demand for synodical sessions. Davidek was convinced that the time had come for at least a small part of the church – in this case the local hidden church in Czechoslovakia – to understand 'the signs of the time' (the so-called *kairos*, the blessed time) and to discuss the position of women within the church.

Davidek was firmly convinced that the local church had the right to call a pastoral synod. His conviction was grounded in his study of the documents of Vatican II, which he further elaborated and interpreted in a very original way. He described his work in the following words:

I believe that this Pastoral Synod deals with a concrete and necessary practice in a given region. Different regions have different problems – it has been so since the beginning of the church. Now, we have the basic directive: what to do for salvation and how to do it best at a certain place. The Synod covers all Czecho-Slovak churches plus seventy-two Czech parishes from Romania and settled in this country. The pastoral realm of our synod consists of the sectors of Bohemia, Moravia, and Slovakia and concerns three (possibly four) rites. Furthermore, we must bear in mind that the synod is not territorial (not related to any diocese). In ecclesiology, the basic emphasis is laid on calling (the mission of the church). Nowadays, each parish community represents a perfect church because Christ is present in it and the connection with the pope is maintained. Two conditions are necessary for a schism: a deliberate break from Rome and an agreement by both sides. This is the aspect of *votum ecclesiae*, which I consider very important. The pope is not the whole church, just as you and I are not the whole church. Therefore, canonical excommunication only concerns individuals in the state of *contra dogmatum*, not the extending of orthodox practices. Everything related to the salvation of souls belongs to the orthodox practice . . . Magisterium is also characteristic of the whole church, though it legally extends only to the bishops. The vocation to teach is ascribed to the whole church. The entire church is infallible. Therefore I consider the dogmatic aspect to be the fundamental premise.[2]

Davidek assumed that 'society needs the service of women as a special tool for the consecration of humankind'.[3] This conclusion was a result of his studies of the history of the church and of his reading of theological treatises, mainly Anglo-Saxon. Davidek's view was moulded not only by the influence of his studies, but also by his experience in the prosecuted church during the 1950s and by his performance of the church's sacramental functions when he was in detention. Of course, Davidek's ideas about the ordination of women were not formed during the six weeks preceding the opening of the Synod but represent the conclusions of his thinking from previous years. This is corroborated by some of his private lectures and seminars (e.g. on celibacy and sacraments), prepared within the framework of secret theological studies.

Davidek's lecture on the ordination of women, probably privately delivered during 1970 is a notable example of his originality. In this lecture, Davidek insists that women have been excluded from ordination only for the last 1000 years. He believes that the final formation of the College of Cardinals in the tenth and eleventh centuries forced a centralization of power. This move was necessarily brought about by the demoralization of the clergy, retaliatory murders among the families from which popes and bishops came, and military expeditions. In addition, at that time . . . the definite norms of the Code of Canon Law (CIC) were formulated, which caused the division between the Western and Eastern rites and their codes.

Davidek suggests that the ruling out of women from ordination (including lower ordination) has no foundation in dogma. Sometimes the words of St Paul are quoted as dogmatic reasons (women should be silent in the church, women should be subordinate to men), but Davidek considers these opinions of Paul merely admonitions or appeals formulated with regard to the particular situation in Corinth. For Davidek, the texts of fundamental importance confirm that St Paul was not against women. On the contrary, he insisted on the equality of women and men (see Galatians 3.28, 'there is neither male nor female . . . you all are one in Christ Jesus'). Davidek also refers to the text of the Acts of the Apostles (1.1–2.6), highlighting the fact that women 'were not overlooked in the choice of the apostle Matthew with the help of the Holy Spirit'. Davidek's lecture takes into consideration the theological aspects of the ordination of women, together with the philosophical and sociological contexts of this issue (in this lecture we come across Davidek's favourite term 'neolithic thinking', which in his view degraded women and should be firmly opposed).

Davidek's views on the position of women in the church also drew upon the foreign literature available at that time, to which he had access mainly in Polish translations. It seems that one of the pieces that most inspired him was the article 'The Place of Women in Ecclesiastical Offices' by Jan Peters. In it the author analysed the role of women in the Old and New Testaments, defined the office of priest historically, and investigated the question why women were precluded from it. Peters also concentrated on looking for the place of women in the sacred office in contemporary theology. This article formulated three premises that were in accordance with Davidek's own deep convictions:

1. From the stance of exegesis we have no decisive arguments to prevent women from taking the priestly office.
2. The preclusion of women from the priestly office was a result of historical development and therefore this practice is devoid of any absolute value, thus losing its general acceptability.
3. The Christian concept of priesthood as a charismatic vocation and service which replaced the former legal concept also forces the Catholic theologian to search for a place and participation of women in the priestly office and to formulate the question whether women could fulfil their redemptive function in a broader, more biblical, context.[4]

Over and above his theoretical preparation for the synod, Davidek devoted no less attention to its organization. The synod was preceded by preparatory gatherings to put together the plan of the meeting. The draft programme as well as the whole undertaking were bound by a personal oath that was taken by all participants.[5] This oath was intended to secure the undisturbed and safe progress of the Synod and to indicate agreement that the synod should be held. The second gathering was held only a few weeks after the first (the last gathering occurred on 10 December 1970). Simultaneously, assiduous work on the concept of the synod was in progress. Davidek initiated translations of some foreign works and articles and preparations of various presentations and expert assessments on the topic. He also carefully elaborated the main contents of the programme, especially the above-mentioned issues of the position of women in the church and their ordination. The final draft can be summed up in the following points:

1. The church all over the world should feel obliged to respect the *kairos*. (Davidek understands *kairos* as a time of visitation in which God comes with a new sign that human beings recognize as an appeal to create a new reality.) In this case, Davidek understands the problem of ordaining women as the question of enabling them to take part in the management of the church and proclaims the end of the year 1970 as the opportune moment – the *kairos*.

2. The ordination of women in certain circumstances can be defended on pastoral-sociological grounds. (Davidek was well acquainted with conditions in women's prisons and also had had experience of many meetings with prisoners, including Vojtécha A. Hasmandová, the general prioress of the Borromean sisters, who told him of her prison experiences.)

3. The cultural-anthropological aspects of the ordination of women should also be regarded as important. By this point Davidek means that there have been not only substantial changes in the position of women in society but also intrinsic shifts in the process of evolution.

4. The ordination of women is supported by the tradition of the church. (Davidek took into account the fact that in the first centuries of Christianity women performed baptisms, brought the eucharist to the sick and had their own place in the hierarchy.)

5. Consequently, the necessary alterations should be made to canon law. (Davidek was convinced that the Code of Canon Law does not cover all possibilities and circumstances that may occur.)[6]

Davidek intended to assemble at the synod the bishops and priests of the so-called 'second line',[7] together with the representatives of congregations and religious orders and, of course, laity. The proportion of clerics and members of religious orders to laity should have been approximately two to one. However, it later transpired – after the oaths were taken at the gatherings – that not all of Davidek's nearest work associates shared with him the conviction that the main purpose of the synod should be the decision whether women can be allowed to obtain ordination. Bedrich Provaznik, Josef Dvořák and Jiří Pojer, bishops consecrated by Davidek, opposed discussion of the problem at the Synod, thus in effect trying to forestall the meeting. Just before the beginning of the Synod they insisted on calling yet another preparatory gathering at which they demanded that the question of ordaining women should be withdrawn from the programme. However, after this meeting, which was held in a very tense atmosphere, the programme of the synod began according to Davidek's plan.

Bishops Provaznik, Dvořák and Pojer handed over to Davidek *The Memorandum* containing nineteen points that summed up their objections. Here are some of their critical comments from the document:

- The councillors are not properly informed: (*a*) the expert knowledge of the participants is insufficient; (*b*) there is a lack of opposition, experts and *periti*; (*c*) the participants (many of them) were not informed in advance. The majority of the participants did not go through any psychological preparation on the main topic of the Synod.
- The present thesis takes a stand against the current practice of the church.
- It is impossible to separate the theoretical-dogmatic-ecclesiological-biblical solution to the problem from the issue of introducing the ordination of women into practice.
- According to the Codex, the local church is not entitled to make such decisions. We raise no objections to the local church acting against the Codex, but such a step must be justified with weighty reasons. To state as the reason the approaching *parousia* and the theology of *kairos* seems insufficient and therefore we suggest that the reasons be further elaborated and explicated. A man must have serious causes for acting contrary to the existing practice of the church. We insist that decisions concerning this matter can be made only by the college of bishops presided over by the pope as the sole holder of power in the church (cf. *Lumen gentium*).
- The ontological-sacral aspect: the royal priesthood also includes women and we should first explore the (hitherto much neglected)

possibilities given by it. Only then should we proceed with the ordination of women. The priest is never consecrated only for himself; priesthood is always a social function, and the social function of women priests is, in the present situation, doubtful and sociologically unprepared.

- Should people vote for the approaching *parousia* it is likely to be a decision resting on misinformation. A test should be given in which they would answer the question what they imagine the approach of the *parousia* to signify.
- We doubt that *hora urget*. People who hear about the topic for the first time in must not be asked to make decisions. They must be given more time to form their opinions.
- Diplomatic relations could be threatened, which in turn could endanger the existence of the 'second line'.
- A decision in favour of the ordination of women would strengthen the position of the Curia and put the existence of the 'second line' at risk during the future persecution of the Church in some other place and at some other time.
- In our opinion, this is a theology of hazard, not of risk.[8]

In the conclusion of *The Memorandum*, the authors insisted that they were acting in accordance with their consciences. Thus, they were prepared for conflict with Davidek because in their view to holding a synod with this kind of programme imperils the whole hidden church. Despite the opposing attitudes of his nearest colleagues, however, Davidek did not interrupt the preparations of the synod.

The synod was held in a parsonage in Koberice, a small village southeast of Brno, where Josef Klusaček, a friend of Davidek's, was the spiritual leader. Klusaček had already allowed several secret priests of Davidek's circle to perform partially public activities.[9] The Synod itself was attended by some sixty people and took place with strict security measures. By agreement, only approved participants were invited to the synod by the co-ordination centre.[10] Of course, such a great number of people could hardly gather in this small village without the danger of attracting some attention. Davidek therefore devised a plan in advance whereby the participants entered the village individually or in small groups, at given intervals and from different directions.

Influenced by the events preceding the Synod, the atmosphere of the first part of the meeting was very agitated. Those councillors who did not agree with the synod interrupted the discussion and cast doubts on the legitimacy of the assembly. They blamed Davidek for insufficient preparation of the synod and maintained that it would be impossible to solve the problem of ordaining women in the course of the meeting. Bishop Provaziuk, who acted as the spokesperson for the opponents, again demanded that the whole assembly take a vote on whether to withdraw the controversial issue from the synod's programme. In the end, the vote took place, and the participants accepted the programme in its original form. Davidek said in his address that the ordination of women,

> is the reality for which we have gathered here. This means that this issue is an appeal to prayer and an appeal to holiness. Nothing else. Society needs the service of women. In psychological terms, society recognizes that it lacks something: society needs the service of women as a special tool for the consecration of the other half of humankind. The present consecration no longer seems to be enough. Nothing but *consecratio mundi*, the consecration of the world, is our aim.[11]

Individual presentations and their ensuing discussion prolonged the synod well into the night. Most interesting were the speeches of the women present, especially some sisters from religious orders. One sister assessed the theme and the course of the synod as follows:

> As early as 1954 the thought [ordination of women] crossed my mind and was later supported by our chaplain among the students. He encouraged us to pray for this idea and to think about it. Hence the issue is not new to me . . . To the objections of the opposing party that as priest a woman cannot assert herself, and that no priest is ordained for himself but for society, I say, in the present circumstances it is not necessary to consider the activity of the woman-priest in the 'first line'. In my opinion, a woman priest could fully develop her activities only in the 'second line'. I consider the question whether this or that woman feels mature enough for the work irrelevant. Which of the men could say that he is duly prepared for this vocation?[12]

Interesting contributions to the discussion were also made by Jan Blaha, who consecrated Davidek bishop, Jiří Krpalek, and Josef Javora, a married priest who stressed the special role of a wife in the priesthood of her husband in the Greek Catholic practice of consecration.

Not until 5 a.m. on the morning of 26 December 1970 did the assembly have a secret ballot on the possibility of the ordination of women. The vote ended in a tie: after the ballots were counted, half the participants wanted the ordination of women and half did not. When the voting process was finished, the synod continued with a heated discussion.

The synod was an undertaking into which Davidek threw much of his strength and knowledge. The words of his closing address to the synod bear witness to his personal commitment and exhaustion:

> Though I have little hope of finishing this task, many new impulses have developed. For me in a way the whole affair is over; now somebody else should take it up. I feel that the responsibility of this task (not, in any way, the decision involved) weighs me down. I apologize for saying so, but I am tired, and I am not happy about having to admit it. I bear it as a heavy burden on my shoulders and in a way it is an exercise in overcoming one's laziness. My nearest colleagues know it. Anyway, when new impulses and fresh inspiration came upon me, I considered the matter so urgent that it deserved to be carried out in these six weeks. Because we also worked on a completely different issue and two gatherings were incomplete due to an illness, not everything was put down in a definite way. So much for the explanation of the pressure of time . . .[14]

In the aftermath of the synod, Davidek decided to proceed with the ordination of women. On the day following the end of the synod, he ordained his general vicar Ludmila Javorová priest.[15] Javorová, born in 1931 in Brno, came from a family of ten children. Her father worked as a laboratory technician at the University of Agriculture in Brno; her mother was a housewife. The family soon moved to Chrlice, where she met Davidek's family. Javorová's wish since her youth had been to enter a religious order of Salesian orientation, but she was prevented from doing so when the Communist regime came to power. So she finished her studies at the Business Academy and then took up various jobs (until her retirement, she worked in an ambulance service and as a worker, a secretary, a court clerk, and a custodian in museum exhibitions). The fundamental turning point in her life came with the return of Davidek from prison in 1964. Javorová began to co-operate with him, became his assistant and housekeeper, and gradually took over important tasks relating to the establishment of the hidden ecclesiastical organization Koinotes. Davidek appointed her his vicar general and then, as stated above, he ordained her priest. However, Javorová was not the only woman ordained by Bishop Davidek. There is some evidence that he later ordained five other women.

Davidek was aware that the ordination of women went against the then current Code of Canon Law (CIC of 1913, canon 968.1). Of course it is difficult to determine the immediate impulse that finally drove him to decide to break church discipline and make a move which as bishop he had no right to make. He stated at the synod that he felt it as a matter of his own conscience which was why he had to start to ordain women . . . 'We should never expect that all people will consent to this practice. There must be somebody who passes down to others something that the majority of humankind will progressively learn to accept.'[17] It can only be conjectured that his decision drew, among other sources, upon his philosophical and theological attitudes as influenced by Teilhard de Chardin. Specifically, a prominent place in Davidek's conception of promoting the parousia was given to the notion that everything that happens once in the process of creation remains present in it and contributes to the 'final shaping of the world'. In this sense Davidek assumed the time had come for the ordination of women and that he was the person who had to take the risk and introduce it in practice:

> Today we recognize that indeed under the influence of gnosis and also under the influence of paganism something in the church would be brought to a halt of women could hold the office of deacon in early Christianity but not in the twentieth century. If we want to return to the invigorating sources of the early Christians in everything else, then we must also embrace this part of their practice. Humankind needs the ordination of women and is literally waiting for it. The church should refrain from preventing it.[18]

Davidek violated the rules of the church because he was convinced that 'life is more important than a Codex'. He very often said this in his lectures. In his view 'the order of deeds' comes before the 'order of regulations and given laws'. Only a few people initially knew that Davidek put his intention to ordain women into practice. Among them were the immediate relatives of the consecrated women and perhaps some of the members of the 'co-ordination centre' of Koinotes (e.g. in the case of the ordination of Javorova it was Jiří Krpalek, whom Davidek later ordained bishop). The majority of the members of Koinotes, including its bishops, only learnt about the ordinations as late as the beginning of the 1990s. Despite the fact that Davidek's ordination of women priests and deacons remained virtually unknown, the theoretical solution to the issue as presented at the synod brought about many problems that Davidek had to face. The most serious of these problems was the opposition of his closest associates, which led to the collapse of

Koinotes and in turn to the weakening of the whole structure of the hidden church. The controversial aspects of the ordination of women in the local church began to be felt even more sharply after Davidek had introduced it into practice. The structure and nature of the communities created by Davidek was not ready to allow women to perform the specific diaconal or priestly functions especially liturgical rites. The Koinotes community was not, and could not be, prepared to accept the ordination of women.

Thus Davidek found himself at odds not only with church laws and practice but also, to a large extent, with the mentality of the majority of active members of Koinotes. Furthermore, Davidek himself had no clear idea about how to proceed in this situation and what role the consecrated women could play in the concrete life of the local church. He was confident about the theological-historical justification for the changes in the church practice which, from the standpoint of his theology of the parousia, was the most vital prerequisite for the ordination of women. On the other hand, he was obviously at a loss regarding the use of the ordination of women. An attempt to formulate the task of women in Koinotes was represented by the holding of the so-called Second Synod, which took place during August 1973 in Cernevy Důl.[19] This meeting was organized mainly by the women active in Koinotes, and its main topic was the outlining of a liturgy that could be adapted to the woman as the bearer of the priestly service. However, the Second Synod at Cerveny Dôl is not remembered by its participants as a decisive event in the history of the hidden church comparable to the Synod in Koberice.

From the above-mentioned problems, it follows that the consecration of women was not of such practical importance as had formerly been hoped for by Davidek and the ordained women. In the end the ordination of women, prepared for and realized by Davidek, undoubtedly under the influence of the atmosphere prevalent during the late 1960s, remained an isolated attempt that nobody in the hidden church either repeated or developed. To be sure, the failure to gain a wider following for the ordination of women was also brought about by the change of atmosphere throughout the church and in the social climate of Czechoslovakia. Perhaps the lack of support for his cause may have been the reason why Davidek did not keep his original promise to Javorová at her ordination to inform the pope about the whole affair. As a result of these factors, Davidek did not work with the ordained women in a manner appropriate to the situation and did not appoint anyone to supervise them, as he usually did in other cases. The ordained women found themselves in isolation and were left to develop their vocation alone. Eventually some of these women ceased to affirm their ordination. Thus, the ordination of women in Koinotes remained a symbolic act and a precedent that was not put to practical use inside the community. To a large extent it went unexplored.

Notes

1. The text of this article is chosen and adapted from the second impression of Petr Fiala and Jiří Hanuś, *Koinotes. Felix M. Davidek and the Hidden Church*, Brno 1997.

2. Recording of the Pastoral Synod. Davidek's closing address delivered on 26 December 1970. Ludmila Javarová's private archive.

3. Notes of Davidek's lecture 'On the Ordination of Women', typescript (August 1970). Ludmila Javarová's private archive.

4. Jan Peters, 'The Place of Women in Ecclesiastical Offices', translation of an article from *Concilium* 1963/4: *Apostolic Succession*, 1963. The Koinotes archive.

5. The text of the oath ran: 'I am aware that all my deeds are subject to the order of the virtue of caution. Therefore in present circumstances I agree, of my own free will, that everything concerning this council of the People of God (i.e. the place, time and contents of the meeting, the participants and the results, both positive and negative) belong to the all-encompassing notion of "secret" for the time being. The contents of the secret I will keep in full with the help of God unless a concrete authority in charge of the Council or his rightful deputy gives an order to do otherwise. Regarding the complexity of the situation, I am also aware that if prosecuted I can be interrogated about this Council. In that case, I am aware that it is God's command both to keep the secret and to speak the truth (i.e. to reveal the truth at a concrete moment in such a way that it could not be misused). This conflict I alone shall try to solve with the help of the Holy Spirit and from now on I shall pray for a successful result. Once more, I declare that I am aware of the need to be silent about the proceedings of the Council, and in these circumstances I swear on the Gospel and before the present witness that with the help of God, I shall keep my promise.' Ludmila Javarová's private archive.

6. Notes taken by Ludmila Javarová during a discussion at the synod. Typescript (970).

7. Within Koinotes, the term 'the second line' denoted the hidden church structure: the priests who performed their office publicly were called 'the first line'.

8. *The Memorandum* (1970). Typescript, Ludmila Javarová's private archive.

9. During major church celebrations, Klusaček led the clandestine priests into the local church before it opened. The priests were 'hidden' in the confessionals and, unseen by anyone, could hear confessions.

10. The group of F. M. Davidek's closest associates, mainly bishops, to whom Davidek various tasks of co-ordination and who acted as his advisory committee.

11. Transcription of several selected passages from Davidek's address to the synod. Typescript, archive of Petr Fiala and Jiří Hanuś.

12. Recording of the contributions to the discussion at the Synod.

13. The synod is preserved on a tape recording lasting several hours.

14. Recording of the Pastoral Synod. Davidek's closing address of 26 December 1970. Ludmila Javarová's private archive.

15. See 'An Interview with Ludmila Javorová', in *Siard*, Bulletin for the parishioners of Julianov, Vinohrady and Zidenice, No. 2, 4 February 1996.

16. In his decision Davidek probably drew on the formulation that allegedly granted special rights to Jan Blaha and, according to Ludmila Javorová, conveyed the meaning that as bishop he should do whatever he believed necessary for the local church. Davidek took his authorization in a very broad sense and therefore felt entitled to perform non-standard episcopal rites as well.

17. Selected quotations from Davidek's speeches to the synod in Koberice (1970). Ludmila Javarová's private archive.

18. Ibid.

19. Material relating to the Second Synod is confused and incomplete. We primarily drew here upon the testimonies of Ludmila Javorová and Jiří Krpalek.

Contributors

HERMANN HÄRING was born in 1937 and studied theology in Munich and Tübingen; between 1969 and 1980 he worked at the Institute of Ecumenical Research in Tübingen; since 1980 he has been Professor of Dogmatic Theology at the Catholic University of Nijmegen. His books include *Kirche und Kerygma. Das Kirchenbild in der Bultmannschule*, 1972; *Die Macht des Bösen. Das Erbe Augustins*, 1979; *Zum Problem des Bosen in der Theologie*, 1985; he was co-editor of the *Wörterbuch des Christentumis*, 1988, and has written articles on ecclesiology and christology, notably in the *Tijdschrift voor Theologie*.

Address: Katholieke Universiteit, Faculteit der Godgeleerdheid, Erasmusgebouw, Erasmusplein 1, 6525 HT Nijmegen, Netherlands.

ISABEL GÓMEZ ACEBO is married with six children. She holds degrees in Political Science and Theology and lectures in theology at the Pontifical University of Comillas in Madrid. Her works include *Dios también es madre* (God is also Mother, 1994, trans. into Italian and Portuguese); 'Esperanza' (Hope) in *10 Mujeres escribieron teología* (Ten women wrote theology, 1993); 'El cuerpo de la mujer y la tierra' (Woman's body and land), in M. Navarro (ed.), *El cuerpo de la mujer* (1996). She is editor-in-chief of the series *En Clave de Mujer* (In Woman's Key), of which six titles have been published in Spain.

Address: Universidad Pontificia Comillas, Hoyos del Espino 14, Madrid, Spain.

LEONARDO BOFF was born in 1938 and for more than twenty years was Professor of Systematic Theology in Petrópolis, Brazil. Since then, he has been Professor of Ethics and Philosophical Ecology at the University of Rio de Janeiro. He is the author of more than sixty books, many of which have been published in English, including *Church: Charism and*

Power (1983); *Trinity and Society* (1989); *New Evangelization: Good News to the Poor* (1992); *The Path to Hope* (1993); *Ecology: Cry of the Land, Cry of the Poor* (1996).

Address: C.P. 92144–25.741–970 Petrópolis, RJ, Brazil.
E-mail: mm-lboff@compuland.com.br

GREGORY BAUM was born in Berlin in 1923; since 1940 he has lived in Canada. He studied at McMaster University in Hamilton, Ontario; Ohio State University; the University of Fribourg, Switzerland; and the new School for Social Research in New York. He is Professor Emeritus at the Religious Studies, Faculty of McGill University, Montreal. He is editor of *The Ecumenist*. His recent books are *Essays in Critical Theology* (1994), *Karl Polanyi on Ethics and Economics* (1996), and *The Church for Others: Protestant Theology in Communist East Germany* (1996).

Address: McGill University, 3520 University Street, Montreal, PQ, H3A 2A7, Canada.

MARY CONDREN was born in Hull and studied at the University of Hull, Boston College and Harvard University, where she graduated with a doctorate in Religion, Gender and Culture. She is the author of many articles on feminist theory, spiritual and liberation theology and has written *The Serpent and the Goddess: Women, Religion and Power in Celtic Ireland*, London 1989. She is currently the Director of the Institute for Feminism and Religion in Ireland, the aim of which is 'to reclaim religion by engaging theoretically and experientially with the issues of feminist theology, ritual, spirituality and ethics'. She is a Research Associate in Women's Studies at Trinity College, Dublin.

Address: 30 Parkhill Rise, Kilmanagh, Dublin 24, Ireland.

ELISABETH SCHÜSSLER FIORENZA is Krister Stendahl Professor at Harvard Divinity School, Massachusetts. She is a past president of the Society of Biblical Literature and founding editor of the *Journal of Feminist Studies in Religion*; she is committed to women-church. Her most recent books are *In Memory of Her: A Feminist Theological Reconstruction of Early Christian Origins*, *The Book of Revelation:*

Judgment and Justice, Bread not Stone: The Challenge of Feminist Biblical Interpretation, and *Jesus: Miriam's Child, Sophia's Prophet.*

Address: The Divinity School, Harvard University, 451 Francis Avenue, Cambridge, MA 02138, USA.

HEDWIG MEYER-WILMES was born in 1953. She studied Catholic theology, pedagogics and German in Münster and then worked as a teacher of religion and a parish assistant before lecturing in theology at the Catholic University in Nijmegen. She is a visiting professor in women's studies and theology at the Catholic University of Leuven and is also President of the European Society for Women's Theological Research. She has written *Rebellion on the Borders*, Kampen 1995, and edited *Over hoeren, taarten en vrouwen die vorbijgaan*, Kampen 1992 (with Lieve Troch), and *Zwischen lila und lavendel*, Regensburg 1996.

Address: Erasmusplein 1, NL 6526 NT, Nijmegen, The Netherlands.

MELANIE A. MAY is Dean of Women and Gender Studies and Professor of Theology at Colgate Rochester Divinity School, Rochester, New York. An ordained minister in the Church of the Brethren, she is a member of the World Council of Churches Standing Commission on Faith and Order and served as Chair of the National Council of Churches (USA) Commission on Faith and Order, 1988–1995. Among her publications are *A Body Knows: A Theopoetics of Death and Resurrection*, New York 1995, and *Bonds of Unity: Women, Theology and the Worldwide Church*, Atlanta 1989, together with numerous articles in journals and edited volumes.

Address: Colgate-Rochester Divinity School, 1100 South Goodman Street, Rochester, NY 14620, USA.

MARY E. HUNT is a feminist theologian from the Roman Catholic tradition active in the women-church movement. She is co-founder and co-director of the Women's Alliance for Theology, Ethics and Ritual (WATER), an educational organization in Silver Spring, MD, USA. She is an adjunct faculty member of the Women's Studies Program at

Georgetown University. She is author of *Fierce Tenderness: A Feminist Theology of Friendship*.

Address: Women's Alliance for Theology, Ethics and Ritual (WATER) 8035 13th Street, Silver Spring, MD 20910, USA.
E-mail: mhunt@hers.com

PETR FIALA teaches political science and history and is head of the Political Science Department at the Faculty of Arts, Masaryk University, Brno. He is also President of the Centre for Democracy and Culture Studies there. He has written books on Catholicism and Politics (1995) and German Political Science (1995).

JIŘÍ HANUŠ teaches church history in the Faculty of Arts, Masaryk University, Brno and the Institute of Ecumenical Studies in Prague. He is editor-in-chief of the *Theological Quarterly*. Together with Petr Fiala he wrote a book about the secret church, *Koinotes* (1994).

Address: Centrum pro Studium Demokracie a Kultury, Mendlovo Nám 1a, 60300 Brno, Czechoslovakia.

The editors wish to thank the following colleagues who contributed in a most helpful way to the final project for this issue.

M. Althaus Reid	Edinburgh	Scotland
N. A. Ančić	Split	Croatia
J. Argüello	Managua	Nicaragua
J. A. Coleman	Los Angeles	America
K. Derksen	Utrecht	The Netherlands
C. Duquoc	Lyons	France
F. Elizondo	Madrid	Spain
V. Elizondo	San Antonio	America
M. Fabri dos Anjos	Sao Paulo	Brazil
I. Fischer	Bonn	Germany
R. Gibellini	Brescia	Italy
M. Hunt	Silver Spring	America
B. van Iersel	Nijmegen	The Netherlands
W. G. Jeanrond	Lund	Sweden
U. King	Bristol	England
H. Lepargneur	Sao Paulo	Brazil
M. J. Mananzan	Manila	Philippines
E. McDonagh	Maynooth	Ireland
N. Mette	Münster	Germany
F. Morrisey	Ottawa	Canada
J. Porter	Nashville	America
P. Richard	San José	Costa Rica
P. Schotsmans	Leuven	Belgium
D. Singles	Lyons	France
L. Sowle Cahill	Chestnut Hill	America
C. Theobald	Paris	France
L. Troch	Breda	The Netherlands
M. Vidal	Madrid	Spain
F. Wilfred	Madras	India

Concilium 1990-1999

1990

1   On the Threshold of the Third Millennium   *The Concilium Foundation*
2   The Ethics of World Religions and Human Rights   *Hans Küng and Jürgen Moltmann*
3   Asking and Thanking   *Christian Duquoc and Casiano Floristan*
4   Collegiality put to the Test   *James Provost and Knut Walf*
5   Coping with Failure   *Norbert Greinacher and Norbert Mette*
6   1492-1992: The Voice of the Victims   *Leonardo Boff and Virgil Elizondo*

1991

1   The Bible and Its Readers   *Wim Beuken, Sean Freyne and Anton Weiler*
2   The Pastoral Care of the Sick   *Mary Collins and David Power*
3   Aging   *Lisa Sowle Cahill and Dietmar Mieth*
4   No Heaven without Earth   *Johann Baptist Metz and Edward Schillebeeckx*
5   *Rerum Novarum*: 100 Years of Catholic Social Teaching   *Gregory Baum
          and John Coleman*
6   The Special Nature of Women   *Anne Carr and Elisabeth Schüssler Fiorenza*

1992

1   Towards the African Synod   *Giuseppe Alberigo and Alphonse Ngindu Mushete*
2   The New Europe   *Norbert Greinacher and Norbert Mette*
3   Fundamentalism as an Ecumenical Challenge   *Hans Küng and Jürgen Moltmann*
4   Where is God?   *Christian Duquoc and Casiano Floristan*
5   The Tabu of Democracy in the Church   *James Provost and Knut Walf*
6   The Debate on Modernity   *Claude Geffré and Jean-Pierre Jossua*

1993

1   Messianism through History   *Wim Beuken and Anton Weiler*
2   Any Room for Christ in Asia?   *Leonardo Boff and Virgil Elizondo*
3   The Spectre of Mass Death   *David Power and Kabasele Lumbala*
4   Migrants and Refugees   *Dietmar Mieth and Lisa Sowle Cahill*
5   Reincarnation or Resurrection?   *Hermann Häring and Johann Baptist Metz*
6   Mass Media   *John Coleman and Miklós Tomka*

1994

1   Violence against Women   *Elisabeth Schüssler Fiorenza and Mary Shawn Copeland*
2   Christianity and Cultures   *Norbert Greinacher and Norbert Mette*
3   Islam: A Challenge for Christianity   *Hans Küng and Jürgen Moltmann*
4   Mysticism and the Institutional Crisis   *Christian Duquoc and Gustavo Gutiérrez*
5   Catholic Identity   *James Provost and Knut Walf*
6   Why Theology?   *Claude Geffré and Werner Jeanrond*

1995

1 The Bible as Cultural Heritage *Wim Beuken and Seán Freyne*
2 The Many Faces of the Divine *Hermann Häring and Johann Baptist Metz*
3 Liturgy and the Body *Louis-Marie Chauvet and François Kabasele Lumbala*
4 The Family *Lisa Sowle Cahill and Dietmar Mieth*
5 Poverty and Ecology *Leonardo Boff and Virgil Elizondo*
6 Religion and Nationalism *John Coleman and Miklós Tomka*

1996

1 Feminist Theology in Different Contexts *Elisabeth Schüssler Fiorenza and M. Shawn Copeland*
2 Little Children Suffer *Maureen Junker-Kenny and Norbert Mette*
3 Pentecostal Movements as an Ecumenical Challenge *Jürgen Moltmann and Karl-Josef Kuschel*
4 Pilgrimage *Virgil Elizondo and Seán Freyne*
5 From Life to Law *James Provost and Knut Walf*
6 The Holy Russian Church and Western Christianity *Giuseppe Alberigo and Oscar Beozzo*

1997

1 Who Do You Say That I Am? *Werner Jeanrond and Christoph Theobald*
2 Outside the Market No Salvation? *Dietmar Mieth and Marciano Vidal*
3 The Church in Fragments: Towards What Kind of Unity? *Giuseppe Ruggieri and Miklós Tomka*
4 Religion as a Source of Violence? *Wim Beuken and Karl-Josef Kuschel*
5 The Return of the Plague *José Oscar Beozzo and Virgil Elizondo*

1998

1 The Fascination of Evil *David Tracy and Hermann Häring*
2 The Ethics of Genetic Engineering *Maureen Junker-Kenny and Lisa Sowle Cahill*
3 Women's Sacred Scriptures *Kwok Pui-Lan and Elisabeth Schüssler Fiorenza*
4 Is the World Ending? *Sean Freyne and Nicholas Lash*
5 Illness and Healing *Louis-Marie Chauvet and Miklós Tomka*

1999

1 Unanswered Questions *Dietmar Mieth and Christoph Theobald*
2 Frontier Violations: The Beginnings of New Identities *Felix Wilfred and Oscar Beozzo*
3 The Non-Ordination of Women and the Politics of Power *Elisabeth Schüssler Fiorenza and Hermann Häring*
4 Faith in a Culture of Self-Gratification *Maureen Junker-Kenny and Miklós Tomka*
5 2000: Reality and Hope *Jon Sobrino and Virgil Elizondo*

CONCILIUM

The Theological Journal of the 1990s

Now available from Orbis Books

Founded in 1965 and published five times a year, *Concilium* is a world-wide journal of theology. Its editors and essayists encompass a veritable 'who's who' of theological scholars. Not only the greatest names in Catholic theology, but also exciting new voices from every part of the world, have written for this unique journal.

Concilium exists to promote theological discussion in the spirit of Vatican II, out of which it was born. It is a catholic journal in the widest sense: rooted firmly in the Catholic heritage, open to other Christian traditions and the world's faiths. Each issue of *Concilium* focusses on a theme of crucial importance and the widest possible concern for our time. With contributions from Asia, Africa, North and South America and Europe, *Concilium* truly reflects the multiple facets of the world church.

Now available from Orbis Books, *Concilium* will continue to focus theological debate and to challenge scholars and students alike.

Concilium Subscription Information - outside North America

Individual Annual Subscription (five issues): £25.00

Institution Annual Subscription (five issues): £35.00

Airmail subscriptions: add £10.00

Individual issues: £8.95 each

New subscribers please return this form:
for a two-year subscription, double the appropriate rate

(for individuals)   £25.00   (1/2 years)   . . . .

(for institutions)   £35.00   (1/2 years)   . . . .

Airmail postage
outside Europe +£10.00   (1/2 years)   . . . .

Total . . . .

I wish to subscribe for one/two years as an individual/institution
(delete as appropriate)

Name/Institution . . . .

Address . . . .

. . . .

. . . .

I enclose a cheque for . . . . payable to SCM Press Ltd

Please charge my Access/Visa/Mastercard no. . . . .

Signature . . . . .Expiry Date . . . .

Please return this form to:
SCM PRESS LTD 9 - 17 St Albans Place London N1 0NX